...ing up quickly. Your voc... you really
larger + larger each day and you
charming "performer" and personali...
proud of you and love you clearly
It is rewarding and c...
have established such a strong bo...
look forward to seeing you often and watching you
grow into a very special young man.
your "NaNa" and I will be there
to share the coming new year with you and we are
looking to enjoy some more hot chocolate with you.
Tell your parents not to work too hard. They are
doing a great job with you!!
Love,
Grandpa + NaNa

...as a young pers...
...is a mature a...
...87 years on ear...
...to that number

I chose...
this letter bec...
much move...
...nal a...

...speaki...
...il you...
your speaking vo...
is very impressive for
a boy your age and
I love how well
you enjoy "flowers".
Enjoy all the
plants & flowers but
...n't abuse them. you
...e very gentle with
Barry

Jaden Miller
724

Dear Jaden,
I am enclosing some
letters I received from childr...
you. Some day you will write
own letters.
I hope you enjoy my
Love Perf...
he is...
...ses this
...uate. In
...d who uses
...s (her) own

STANLEY SEIDMAN

5/18/15
Re: The Loss of a lo...
Dear Jaden,
I just learned from your mother th...
...me very upset when you witnessed h...
...peared when she shared with you th...
...ayley's sister was terminally ill a...
prospect of death at such an...
your emotional response was
...this unhappy occurence...
...e to share my thoughts w...
an eventuality that all...
having an understa...
...important one...

...express my feel...
...because I want you...
...(which we all must face)...
...e on this earth to help...
...cept. It is vital for you t...
...stand why it is so importan...
...of love for yourself and others...
...sincere attempt to make the worl...
...follow you. This approach...
...worthwhile a...

Principles & Parables

Correspondence Between
Grandfather & Grandson

Stan Seidman & Jaden Miller

with
Regina Miller

Published by Regina Miller
Copyright © 2016 Stanley Seidman, Jaden Miller, Regina Miller

Book Design by Lisa Occhipinti/Logette

DEDICATION

Principles and Parables is dedicated
to everyone that ever took the
time to write a letter to
someone they loved.

Jaden would love to dedicate
this book to his Papa!

Contents

My dad, Stan Seidman, has the softest, calmest voice that ever commanded a room. When he talks, people listen. He has also made brilliant use of his wisdom and humor through writing. Over the years, I've treasured the handwritten letters he has sent me. They still teach and comfort me, especially during challenging times.

I'm not the only one Stan's love and guidance has touched. For over sixty years, he worked hard as an educator and leader in public and private schools in New York City. He took uncompromising stands on important issues affecting students and teachers of all experiences and talents. Now that "Principal Seidman" is on Facebook, he has reconnected with over six decades' worth of students, families, and colleagues.

So, how could such an accomplished, dedicated, and beloved man have suddenly felt lonely and disconnected, a few years ago?

One word: retirement.

Since Stan has profound insights about society, education, and parenting, and his online following still had a great interest in learning from him, I suggested that he write a book. However, all the encouragement of family and former students could not overcome his reluctance.

Meanwhile, 3,000 miles away, my son Jaden was in the fourth grade.

Jaden is a gift in every sense of the word — sensitive, funny, observant, and always thrilled to learn more about the world and the people around him. Who better to receive Principal Seidman's wisdom? And what better way to share it with the next generation than through letter writing?

When I asked my dad to start writing letters to Jaden, we decided I would offer up subjects inspired by a current incident or challenge in our household. Stan would then address and expand upon the themes. For example, during a period in which Jaden was upset I couldn't be home all the time, my dad wrote him a letter titled, "Why it is Cool That Your Mom Works." (page 86). Of course, that remains one of my favorites!

My dad was out of his doldrums. The idea of a book had taken hold. But would a simple collection of letters do justice to his wit and insights? And how could it be organized in a compelling way?

As often happens, the answers came unexpectedly. This past summer, a beloved relative passed away after battling cancer, Stan wrote to Jaden a letter titled "The Loss of a Loved One" (page 13). By this time, we had a ritual at home. Jaden would open the envelope, each of us would read the letter privately and a conversation would follow from dinner until bedtime. The morning after we received my dad's thoughts on loss, something changed. Jaden wrote his own letter—a response, to send to his Papa! I was so touched that my dad and Kim, even in her passing, had inspired my then 9-year-old son to share his own ideas in a handwritten letter.

As Jaden and Stan took up the ancient art of letter writing, I quickly realized that this would be a rich exercise in creativity and self-discovery for both of them. There are no rules to letters, no abbreviations, no acronyms and certainly no 140 character limit. It would take proper reflection and guidance but if Jaden found those on this journey, there are many more things he would find: a voice, a guide to life, and a grandfather's incredible life story.

I wanted to create this book to share the blessings of a 12 year old regularly trading letters with his 87 year old grandfather. It's a wonderful reminder that wisdom comes to us in many ways. We hope you find something of value, whether it's a new perspective or timeless principles offered by a brilliant man who still commands the room.

Regina Miller

PREFACE

This letter writing experience has taken me through the mind and being of my papa, Stan Seidman. I have learned so much about him and his perspective. He has so much to share with the world. He has been through lots of different experiences in his long lifetime that should be told.

I love his passion for writing. It has made him a happier person and helped him find what he loved (other than his wife, AKA my nana). I have learned many different things during our time writing each other letters. He taught me many good life lessons that have helped me change into a more mature and understanding person.

When I write letters to my Papa, it makes me feel involved in his life. I enjoy having these long distance conversations with him. When I read the letters he writes, I am amazed at the things he elaborates on. One of my favorite letters is on "Learning How to Lose" (page xx). I used to be a sore loser. After I read that letter, I applied the things he said. Now I am a better sport and still look for the fun in the games even if I lose. I still hate losing because I am competitive, but now when I lose I am more calm than I ever was before.

At first, I honestly didn't want to start writing letters. I was very lazy and didn't want to do any hard work. I only started to do the writing because of my mom. I know she loves her dad, and I wanted to make her happy. This was the initial reason for me to write. But, over time, I began to love writing back to my Papa. I love talking to him because he offers so much wisdom and perspective on the world. I also realized that these writing conversations are very important to him and me. I rarely see him, so when we write each other it unites us again. We live 3000 miles away from each other, but we have never been closer.

I want to make sure that everyone reading this book will pay attention to my papa's stories and lessons. Papa was a great school teacher and principal and will always be remembered by his students, but I feel that this book could be his legacy as a person. Many people could learn life lessons and tools to help them during their own lives because of this book. My papa has written not only his words in these letters, but has written a piece of his heart in them as well. He has spent lots of time and effort writing his "words of wisdom" to me, and I hope they will help you as well.

Jaden Miller

INTRODUCTION:
THE FIRST LETTER

Dear Jaden,

I am going to attempt to write a letter to you on a regular basis for as long as I am able. This coming March (2014) I will be reaching my 85th birthday and I thought that this might be a good time for me to share some of the experiences I enjoyed as a boy growing up, as a man trying to be mature in making decisions, as a parent raising two developing daughters, as a teacher trying to impart knowledge to receptive children and being a school administrator trying to create an environment for all the members of a school community to function as a growing and caring body of people whose first commitment would be to the welfare of children. Since you are my only grandchild, I feel that the exchange of ideas and thoughts with you might be of value for the both of us.

This is not being written because I feel that I have all the answers to the many questions we all have to face in life, but that I am hopeful that by sharing my positive and negative experiences of growing up and learning might be of some benefit to you as you grow and mature into adulthood.

I truly love and care for you very much. You are a remarkably fortunate boy who will someday grow into a mature, athletic and bright young man. You did a good job in "choosing" your parents (small joke) and they have to enjoy a happy, productive life.

Next week I will write you about a topic close to my heart. We will look closely at the meaning of "intelligence" (being smart) and explore the different forms of intelligence and the responsibilities and issues that surround this subject. You are welcomed to write me back if you would like to communicate your ideas to me. If not, we can always speak to each other on the telephone or in person.

Take good care of yourself and regards and love to your mom and dad.

Love,
Papa & of course, Nana
September 20, 2013

hood, I have decided to change

vn. Since your "voyage" is present

nerging and my narrative (story)

felt the need to share it with

vould serve to provide you with som

und of experiences that reflects u

going to divide this experience in

of all, in this letter I will mak

share my feelings and thoughts

he field of education which covev

us and occupied a major part of

nent (later) letter I will attempt to

gs, emotions and thoughts about wh

eevson, as a husband and father and

adult who has been blessed with

earth and who is looking forward

ser.

se to write to you about my care

secause it was a major part of my li

ove factual and easier to expand

and move intimate part of who I

voluing person requires a bit move

y part- In other words, this p

s experience is easier for me to

CHAPTER 1

Setting a Course

Letters on Life Skills

Dear Jaden,

Since I was having a "bad" day today I thought it might be a good idea to share some of my thoughts about how to deal with this issue with you since it is something that all of us face at various times in our lives. Learning how to deal with this problem would be a good one for us to explore together. One of the most important skills for all of us to learn is how to develop the necessary resilience (ability to bounce back) when things are not going well for you. We all have "bad days" or face difficult circumstances that will test us as we grow and develop.

When things are not going well for people they need to establish strategies to deal with whatever the difficulty might be. First, you need to understand that time usually provides an opportunity for feelings of anger, illness, upset and a host of other negative feelings to subside (lessen) simply because time has been provided to allow us to better understand what is upsetting us or making us feel bad or inadequate. Time allows you to rethink your upset and provides you with the opportunity to conduct yourself with more dignity and understanding in dealing with your "bad day". It is alright to have a bad day. If everything was great all the time you would lose perspective (understanding) and appreciation when you are having a "good day". In other words, you need to have some challenges in your life because they will help you appreciate more the times when life is good and everything is going your way. I wish I could tell you that there will be no adversity (difficulty) in your life. Unfortunately, there will be some despair and upset in your life and how you deal with those moments will in many ways determine how successful and rewarding your life on earth will be and how others will evaluate you as a person.

When you are facing a problem that is perplexing (troubling) you it is important not to respond immediately. Since the likelihood is that you will act emotionally and abruptly and say or do something that will worsen the situation and fuel the fire. Take

2

time to think about the situation or better still, remove yourself from it and return at a later time when you are completely under control and are prepared to respond in a manner that will reflect a demeanor (behavior) and considered thinking on your part. Your response as a result will be better received by your antagonist (opponent) or person you have had a disagreement or issue with.

You may not always be right but if you feel strongly about something that is upsetting to you and others then express yourself sincerely and be willing to listen to the other side. In many cases the result will be a compromise where no one wins or loses. You grow to be accepting of both points of view and agree to disagree with respect shown to both points of view.

If you are passionate about your side of any dispute then express yourself with fervor (strength) and make your arguments clear and sincere and hold tight to your beliefs. You do not have to yell or scream to be heard. If you show respect for the other points of view, you should and usually will receive the same for your position.

There will be days when you will be moody or "down" and find it difficult to communicate. That would be a good time to involve yourself in an independent activity (reading, computer work, writing, etc.) and recognize that this feeling will pass and allow you to look forward to being part of a group. Most of us are social human beings, however all of us need quiet and independent time to merely think and "veg" out.

Don't make life anymore complex than it is. Enjoy your good days (which are many) and learn from your infrequent "bad days". Be yourself and enjoy!!

Love,
Papa & Nana
June 5, 2015

Dear Papa,

I really liked your letter on bad days. It's okay to have bad days because it's part of everyday life. Everybody has bad days, but they don't appreciate them. I know you're thinking, "Who does that?" Every bad day we have makes us appreciate the normal days a little bit more.

The days that seem to have nothing going on actually have a lot going on that you don't notice. Something may seem normal to you, but if you stop and take a step back to appreciate what you are looking at, it makes it a lot more special than it would have been to you otherwise. So, when you find yourself at a football game, or see people laughing, maybe even when you look at yourself in the mirror, try to find the deeper levels. A football game at first could be any normal game. But I remember when my parents took me to my first football game. It was a new and exciting day for me because it was when I first developed an interest in football. If you see people laughing, it may be a random bunch of people laughing for no reason. But if you take a closer look, it could be friends that just heard a hilarious inside joke. Also, if you see yourself in a mirror, it could just look like a familiar face. But if you look at it from a profound perspective, you see a person with the potential to do something great. When we look at the deeper level, we find wisdom, happiness, and quality.

Thankfully, there are very special days where fun and awesome things happen. Good days relieve discomfort and feelings like being upset, afraid, or stressed. Since good days come in so many different forms, I thought I would give an example further describing one kind of good day. A good day is when nothing seems to go wrong, where everything seems to be leaning your direction. Sometimes the little things can turn a normal day into

4

a good day: such as reading, relaxing, or doing what you love most. It could be an activity or hobby that can brighten your day. I know you really enjoy gardening. It calms you down and takes away your stress. Others may not enjoy gardening as much as you do, but you have a relationship with gardening that other gardeners may not have. That makes gardening special to you.

Most people don't notice a good day until the end of it, and many people take good days for granted. If somebody keeps having good days, they could start to think that the good days they are having are just normal, casual days. They don't enjoy the happiness of everyday life end up unfulfilled. This is why I try to enjoy the good days, so I am in a good mood and happy. I also try to be resilient on bad days and I bounce back.

Sometimes when I have a bad day it makes me feel better to play basketball or simply just watch TV. These things keep me relaxed so they are a good way for me to make myself feel happier. I think that I am resilient enough to bounce back. I can recover from a bad test score or a problem with a friend. On a test, you can't change a bad grade; what's done is done. If I get a bad test score, I study hard before the next test I take. If you have a problem with a friend, you should try to apologize if you did something wrong, or try and let the whole disagreement roll over. Do what needs to be done when you are having a bad day to turn it into a good day.

I thought your letter was very inspiring and helpful. Your advice was stellar, and I hope this is helpful advice to reduce your bad days and create more good days.

Love,
Jaden

Dear Jaden,

Today I would like to share with you my thoughts about the topic "Becoming Independent" you are now ten years old (going on 35, small joke) and it is time for you to look at this issue and move positively toward accepting this responsibility. This need has evolved as you mature from your early childhood years into your present "pre-teen" stage in your life. You are really growing up rapidly and you've made some remarkable moves toward becoming independent.

As a baby and young child there was a natural and important need for you to be very dependent and clearly connected to your parents. They provided the security and warm feelings and love that make you feel secure about yourself and it helped teach you how to respond to all the people in your environment (family, friends and others). Your personality which includes such things as a sense of humor, a love for others, an ability to work and play with all kinds of people, a sense of security that allows you to explore new and challenging experiences have all formed you. However, you are now reaching a new level in your development. Congratulations! You passed childhood and it is time to take an important step in growing up to the challenge of independence.

You have made a significant step by agreeing to go to a "sleep away" camp this summer. You wisely selected a short period of time (one week) to be away from home and this made this experience a total success for you. With this "under your belt" you can now look forward to extending the period of time you attend camp in the future. Being independent means that your parents have done a good job in preparing you to grow up to be a successful, functioning adult. Their love for you doesn't diminish with time but grows as they observe you in your process toward manhood. They take great pride in your achievements and feel especially good knowing that they have helped to create a young man who will someday make a significant contribution in the world that he lives in as an adult.

Independence means learning to "fend" for yourself by utilizing (using) all the love, teachings, discussions and experiences your parents shared with you as a child growing up. The ages of 10-18 are filled with opportunities for you to mature and become self-sufficient. I like the way you have accepted the challenge of creating a new, appropriate room environment for yourself after you returned from camp. You have really grown to become a truly feeling and good person. Continue to build on that foundation and grow to be the best you can be. That will be more than fine for all of us who love you.

Enjoy your exotic trip next week!

Love,
Papa & Nana
July 2, 2014

EDUCATION

Dear Jaden,

It was great seeing you and spending time with you last week during the holidays, you are really growing up quickly and I am very proud of you and the maturity level you displayed during your visit. It is obvious that you have made great strides in your academic development, but even more than that your growth as a social person and communicator has soared (moved higher) to make you a well-rounded interesting and inviting young person. You should be proud of the strides you have made in that direction and you have my compliments for the progress you have made thus far. I have no doubts that your parents have helped to contribute to this positive movement.

Much of what you have learned academically can be attributed to your school's efforts in assisting you in your growth as a student, but I would also like to share some of my philosophy (thoughts) about the meaning of being educated. Someone once told me "a child who is only educated in school is poorly educated". In other words, schooling is part of the educative process but the body of experiences you are exposed to out of school such as time you spend with parents and friends, devotion to the reading of books and a variety of other materials, having active relationships with all kinds of people, traveling to new and different places and just living a vibrant lifestyle by being open to all kinds of learning opportunities will truly make you an educated person.

You need to make yourself available to all kinds of living experiences to be able to develop into a well rounded, intelligent human being. A key part of your life will center around your social skills and the ability to relate to all kinds of people. Personality is a key part of who you are and who you will be as a functioning person or being. That piece of you will develop and grow as you go through a myriad (large number) of experiences during your entire life.

I would love for you to enjoy a rich life of learning through the process of knowing how to utilize your intelligence and your social skills to make a real contribution to our society. Your new love for reading will expose you to a world of learning that will allow you to gather knowledge and be able to incorporate it into whatever your future destiny might become. You have already taken a great step forward in that direction.

If you are able to take your knowledge and blend it with accepting social skills (for example, being a "people person" like your mother) then your horizons will become unlimited. I urge you to take advantage of the opportunities provided for you and always recognize that there is always more to learn and to share. A truly happy and complete person has the need and the ability to continue to grow. Your future holds great opportunities for you. A truly happy and complete person has the need and the ability to continue to grow. Your future holds great opportunities for you. Take advantage and enjoy them.

Love,
Papa & Nana
January 1, 2016

FADED DREAMS

Dear Jaden,

I understand that recently you became upset about your future aspiration (goal) of becoming a N.B.A basketball player after your coach reprimanded your team for losing an important game. While this game was significant to the coach and the entire team, allow me to remind you that it was only one game and even championship teams lose games. We learn from our losses and move on to improvements. While you are very young to be thinking about your future endeavors in the world of work and the profession you might be interested in as an adult, I applaud you for your thoughts and interests in this area. You are still somewhat young to be overly concerned regarding this issue, however I would like to take this opportunity to spend some time with you in this letter to explore what the future might hold for you if you allow it to unfold.

At this particular time in your life it is important to explore and learn about the many options and opportunities that might be of interest to you before you arrive at any decision pertaining to the occupation or position you will enter as an adult. You have a number of years to go before you reach that level. Right now the thought of becoming a professional basketball player might be alluring (appealing) but it might not be an area that best suits your innate (inborn) skills, abilities, interests and temperament. You will need time and additional maturity to make this long term commitment to a life's work and I encourage you to make "haste slowly" (slow down) in choosing the field of work or profession that will dominate your entire life as an adult next to choosing a mate (wife or significant other) this will be the decision that will determine you as a contributing member of our society.

When I was your age my life centered around my love for baseball. My dream was to become a major league player and might I add that this was the dream of many young people at that time who sought to become future sports heroes similar to the ones that they worshipped. Truthfully, it is the dream of many boys and girls as they grow to maturity. My dream came to an ending when I was invited to a NY Giant's baseball camp when I was 18 years old to "try out" for a minor league team. I thought I was good but soon realized that there were many others like me who were bigger, better and stronger. I left the camp discouraged but pleased that I had this opportunity and I looked forward to redirecting my life to other areas of interest. I enjoyed and began to look to other potential fields of future work possibilities. This experience, as upsetting as it was, allowed me to grow to my next stage in life.

I share this story with you in the expectation that you will use the next ten or more years in your life exploring who you are as a person, what you do best, what your interests and passions are and finally what field of work you will select that will provide you with the greatest satisfaction, reward and love. Take your time in making a decision. Basketball may be great but there will be other opportunities that might fulfill you even more. I found it in the teaching profession, you dad found it in aviation and your mother found it in dancing as a young woman and now in the charitable activities she supervises and coordinates for others. Your call in this area will come in the future.

Life is good if you feel that you have contributed to the welfare of others as well as to yourself. Please take your time and look "far and wide" for Future Life's work. One basketball loss might open enormous possibilities for you as did the rejection I once faced in baseball camp. Take advantage of what you possess as a person and incorporate those strengths into your future chosen profession. Love what you are doing and continue to grow as an individual in all walks of life.

> Love,
> Papa & Nana
> January 22, 2016

GOALS

Dear Jaden,

I was pleased to learn that one of your classroom assignments was to select a "goal" for the school year and to make a decided effort to accomplish it. Your choice of incorporating a positive experience of life as presented by a baseball legend, Bo Jackson into your hopes and expectations for the future was commendable. His aim in life (and now yours) was "to set your goals high and not stop until you got there." I applaud your choice and I would like to take the opportunity to share my thoughts about the need for selecting achievable goals in your life.

Goals are often a reflection of your personality and the inner desires that guide you through the decisions you make as you are growing up. Setting your goals high affords you the opportunity to stretch your horizon while also encouraging you to motivate yourself to a higher level of satisfaction as you grow and develop. I urge you to make your goals personal and not material. You can work to make great "gobs" of money but outside of gaining material wealth there is a strong need to ask yourself, does this goal in your life make you a more productive and better person.

Your goals in life should center around the ingredients that will make your life more meaningful and significant.

When I was a young man I dreamed of becoming a professional baseball player. Many boys harbor a desire similar to mine as they grow to maturity. Sports often play a major role in the loves of boys and girls and it certainly did in my childhood. I grew to learn and realize that in spite of my efforts to reach that lofty goal that was beyond my "skill set" when I had the opportunity to be evaluated by some professional baseball scouts when I was invited for a "try out" in Florida. It was determined that I was a good athlete but the opportunity for me to become a professional in that area was limited. I was disappointed upon hearing that news, but I realized that it now became important for me to set new goals which would help me find a purpose that would give me satisfaction and direction in my future life. I share this with you to let you know that while goals in life can change, you still need whatever those new goals might be. You don't compromise but merely put that some enthusiasm into your newly created aims as you mature.

My new goal emerged when I entered college and decided to become the best educator that I was capable of being. Teaching and school administration became my life's work and as Bo Jackson suggested, " I set my goals high and didn't stop there" during my sixty years devoted to this noble profession. Whatever you choose to do during your life I urge you to follow the philosophy you feel works for you. You've made a strong start in that direction and I wish you well.

Love,
Papa & Nana
September 12, 2014

Dear Jaden,

    I just learned from your mother that you became very upset when you witnessed how sad she appeared when she shared with you that your aunt Hayley's sister was terminally ill and would be facing the prospect of death at such an early stage in her life. Your emotional response was understandable and I felt that this unhappy occurrence might be a good opportunity for me to share my thoughts with you regarding this issue. It is an eventuality that all of us share as human beings and having an understanding of this final act of life is an important one for you to appreciate and recognize.

    I am willing to express my feelings to you about this sensitive issue because I want you to learn to accept this ending of life (which we all must face) as a celebration of our existence on this earth to help you gain an appreciation for this concept. It is vital for you to accept the need to truly understand why it is so important for you to enjoy a lifetime of love for yourself and others and

> *...life continues through the threads we weave and create during our time on earth.*

to make an honest and sincere attempt to make the world a better place for those who follow you. This approach will make your life a more meaningful and worthwhile adventure for yourself and those who share it with you.

    The passing of someone you cared for and felt close to will undoubtably bring a feeling of sorrow to you. This is very natural and normal and tears and upset will accompany this feeling. Yes, even boys (men) are allowed to cry and to express their inner emotions. However, once you have passed through that period of mourning, it is important to recognize that your relationship and connection with the deceased person still remains. Anyone who has lived a life that embraces people (family & friends) around him and who has lived always remain in the hearts and minds of the family and friends they have left behind. It is how you "touched" people and acknowledged their strengths, weaknesses, needs, etc. with kindness and understanding that allow them to never let your spirit die. You leave a part of yourself to all who have grown to cherish the time you spent with them. In that way, you remain an integral part of the world you once occupied.

To make this more personal and relevant to our family, I would like to share my feelings and sentiments about the time (hopefully in the distant future) when your grandmother (nana) and I will no longer be around (physically) with you and your parents. We feel pleased that we will still continue to remain a part of you and others simply because you, your mother and aunt Lil remain part of us due to some of the genes we passed along to all of you and through a history of caring and love which will continue our legacy.

When my parents passed away at a much too early a time in their lives, I strived to keep them alive in my heart and mind and did not allow them to disappear or be forgotten. I have visited them often at the cemetery during the past 65 years and have often seek their support and guidance through prayers. They remain very much alive in my heart. I share this with you not in remorse (sadness) but with the hope that you will grow to understand that life continues through the threads we weave and create during our time on earth.

Love,
Papa & Nana
May 18, 2015

Dear Papa,

Your letter about loss was really moving. It helped especially when Aunt Kim passed. Because I read this letter, it guided me through this tragedy and helped me stay strong. Kim was very nice and always put others before her. I was sad and surprised when I heard she had passed. I didn't know her that well and I wish that I could have known her better. I really thought she would pull through but unfortunately she didn't. I knew this was natural part of life, but a part of me didn't understand why it had to happen so soon.

I truly feel sorry for her kids. I feel sorry for them because now they are obviously sad and hurt, but also they need to keep themselves going. They need to help keep the family together. This may be hard for them because they still may be in the mourning phase. I know you went through this in your life and I would like to know how you felt emotionally, if you felt confident that you could lead your family through that dark time, and if you felt scared of the road ahead.

I thought that what you wrote about recognizing and appreciating the person that has passed was very meaningful. I thought it was comforting how we, as humans, can still remember the good times with the people that are in our lives or live on in our hearts. I think that these words of wisdom will guide me to be strong and prepared for most things -tragic in life – that will be thrown at me. If someone important to me passes no matter how prepared I am I will still be hurt, but after the mourning phase is over I have to recognize and remember the person.

If someone is important to you or you miss them it shows that they made an impact on your life. No matter how big or small, the impact that they made will stick with you forever. I will always remember the time I saw Kim at dinner with my parents and cousins. She was very caring and funny. She made

15

me chuckle when she told my cousin to stop eating so fast like a pig. She would ask if anybody needed anything and always be on the lookout for someone who needs a helping hand. Aunt Kim was a special person that brought happiness to everyone around her.

I would like to dedicate this response and your original letter to Aunt Haley. This has been a tough time and maybe our words would guide her through this part of her life.

Love,
Jaden

MAKING LIFE CHOICES

Dear Jaden,

I thought it might be appropriate to take an abrupt turn in our communications and allow you the opportunity to get to know me a bit better as a person. After writing you a number of letters regarding issues and challenges you might be facing in your development toward adulthood, I have decided to change our course for a brief turn. Since your "voyage" is presently in the process of emerging and my narrative (story) is drawing to an end I felt the need to share it with you in the hope that it would serve to provide you with some understanding of the background of experiences that reflects my life's work. I am going to divide this experience into two sections. First of all, in this letter I will make an attempt to share my feelings and thoughts about my career in the field of education which covered a period of over 60 years and occupied a major part of my life. In a subsequent (later) letter I will attempt to share with you my feelings, emotions and thoughts about who I was as a young person, as a husband and father and finally as a mature adult who has been blessed with at least 87 years on earth and who is looking forward to adding to that number.

I chose to write to you about my career in this letter because it was a major part of my life and it is much more factual and easier to expand upon while the personal and more intimate part of who I am as an evolving person requires a bit more of an effort on my part. In other words, this portion of my life's experience is easier for me to address and the other more personal revealing piece will have more significance for you as a result of the background knowledge you hopefully will gain from this letter.

Allow me to start. At the age of 22 I was appointed as a classroom teacher to Public School #45, a school in Brooklyn whose population was 100% Afro-American and Hispanic. As a beginning teacher it proved to be a huge challenge (38-40 children in a small room, very little supplies, books or teaching materials and absolutely no administrative or supervisory support). I fell in love with my class because they accepted me and all my inadequacies as a teacher but appeared to enjoy my sense of humor and my efforts to make each school day a pleasant experience. They became my "family" and since this teaching assignment followed the unfortunate passing of my parents, it helped to lessen the pain I was feeling at that time. I taught at this school for four years and at the end of each year I cried when I had to say "goodbye" to each class as they moved on to the next grade level. During the time I was at P.S. 45 I grew to feel very strongly that I should prepare myself for the process of becoming a principal of a school. I sincerely felt that I could do a better job at it than my present principal and this feeling motivated me to study for the needed examinations to become a school administrator. There was nothing wrong with my ego at that time. I became a proficient test taker and while I wasn't the brightest student in the world, I was highly motivated and took the necessary courses, attended numerous workshops and wrote answers to questions from previous examinations. I became a "robot" and learned to "beat the game" I gained high marks (grades) on the exams for guidance counselor, supervisor of guidance, assistant principal and eventually principal.

I was assigned as a guidance counselor to two different junior high schools and enjoyed the one-on-one opportunities I engaged in my new capacity. It was rewarding and allowed me time to continue my studies in school administration. I then passed the assistant principal examination with a high score which allowed me to return to P.S. 45 (now P.S. 270) where I started as a teacher. Most of the teachers were older than my parents but they welcomed me back as a "long lost son". I was 27 years old and full of energy, vim and vigor. It became the right move for me as I developed professionally. The same principal was there and he was pleased to give me "free reign" (full authority) to administer to the school's needs. I conducted teacher and parent meetings, observed teachers in the classroom, etc. and this total experience helped to prepare me to become a licensed principal of a school. The early experiences I enjoyed at P.S. 45 allowed me the opportunity to gain insight and understanding of the plight (difficulty) that minority groups faced in meeting the challenges of our society. If I was "liberal" then, I grew more so as I moved forward with my professional pursuits.

A few years later I was fortunate to pass the examination to become a "full fledged" principal in the NYC school system. I attained the 3rd highest score and was offered an assignment to a school in Staten Island (predominantly white population in a middle class environment). I rejected this offer and accepted an appointment to Public School 9 (a school in the same district as P.S. 45 and with a similar population). At the age of 32 I felt that I could "beat the world" and looked forward to this challenge.

P.S. 9 proved to be a stimulating and ideal opportunity for me to continue my professional growth. It also provided the launching point for the many events that symbolized my professional career and provided the momentum for what was to follow. Public School 9 was a huge school with almost 2,000 students, two large buildings and a staff of over 100 teachers and specialists. When I was appointed I was alerted to a strong anti-Semitic sentiment that existed in the school community and much of it was directed and focused on the school and the previous principal who was not well received by the parent body. There was one community meeting that I attended which erupted into a series of fist fights, the throwing of chairs, the locking of doors and lots of screaming to the point of my fearing for my safety. It required numerous meetings and close involvement with the parents to lessen the tension at the school. Hiring additional black teachers and personnel plus the addition of some well received programs relating to Black History and enrichment activities for all the grades helped but the most important factor that made the school become a positive focal point for the community was its response to a school strike that closed the doors of almost every school in NYC. While I believed very strongly in many of the causes promoted by the Union (teachers rights and higher wages) I strongly disagreed with the closing of schools for an extended period of time, particularly in the less advantaged parts of our city such as black communities where there was little or no place for large numbers of children to spend their days away from school while their parents worked, etc. In my mind, schools were a "safe haven" for children and should remain open to meet their many needs. As a result I kept my school open and managed the school with a small number of teachers (mostly minority) and other community members. I was probably the only white, Jewish principal to follow that path. Obviously, I felt very passionate about this issue and brought my own two daughters to school each day (your mother was 4 years old at that time) to emphasize this point.

One day the custodian of the building locked all the gates and doors and the children were left waiting outside in the cold. I was forced to climb the school fence and retrieve the keys to open the gates and doors. The school community remained united and eventually the strike was settled and we returned to normal. There was one major incident and this occurred a day before the strike ended. There were incidents of abuse and fighting reported at some of the schools that remained open. A very large fellow (really a menacing looking thug) visited our school with a number of his friends to "check how the school was doing." While being frightened by him and his friends who were waiting quietly in the lobby, I somehow kept a quiet demeanor and convinced him and his "colleagues" to leave quietly by suggesting that there were other places that could use his service. He smiled at me and left much to my relief. I remained shaken for along time. The strike was over and everything returned to normal throughout the school system although some bad feelings existed for a long time. I spent five years as the head of the school and felt proud of what was accomplished there.

After spending 20 years in schools with large numbers of underprivileged children in low socioeconomic communities, I was motivated to seek a transfer to a school that was 15 minutes from my home (by bicycle) which was located in a middle class neighborhood with a predominant population of white families. The thought of sleeping later in the morning and being able to bicycle to school each day was inviting and I succumbed (gave in) to the lure of easy living. While I enjoyed this new challenge , the school, its parents and children looked forward to my new assignment. I soon learned that the school was located in a rather conservative community that there would be some roadblocks that I didn't anticipate. For most part people in my profession would consider this new appointment a "plum" (sweet) position. During my second year at the school I received a letter from the Community School Board which was mailed to all the principals in the district stating that the state legislature was considering passing a law that would provide recognition and equal rights to all people regardless of their sexual preference and that I should as the head of school notify the parent body that they should not support this bill and urge them to vote against it. I strongly objected to this misuse of my role and I wrote a letter to the Board reflecting that this kind of action was inappropriate and not included in my job description and that people should have their right to express their own beliefs and opinions regarding matters of concern to them. I was reprimanded. It was suggested that I give up my license as principal after I refused to say whether or not I would have a homosexual as a teacher. When I refused to answer this obnoxious question, my own sexuality was questioned and I abruptly departed from this meeting. When the offices of the United Federation of Teachers and the Council of Supervisors were made aware of this situation they offered to provide legal services and support on my behalf. I thanked them for their concern but felt it would not be necessary. I felt strongly that I was merely expressing my legally granted rights and that I didn't do anything that merited the response I received. Two days later I received an "invitation" to meet the chairman of the Community School Board for breakfast at his home. When I entered his home I was overwhelmed by the huge number of framed photographs of US Army Generals (from Washington to Eisenhower) that covered the walls and desks in his house. In addition, there was an abundance of religious artifacts on display throughout the house. It was quite intimidating. I am pleased to inform you that he "forgave" me and said, "Stan, you've been a very bad boy, but I am willing to forgive and forget." I left perplexed (confused) but pleased that it was over.

Fortunately for me I received a call from Hunter College the following week notifying me that a position for the principal of Hunter College Campus School, a school for gifted children was available and that I had been recommended as someone who had experience with ethnically varied school population and that they were looking for a school director to fully implement a mandate that they had received to integrate the school. The school was going through a transition period as it moved from a school that catered to the needs of gifted children who were predominantly white to one that would be more reflective of the racial-ethnic make-up of our city. A former colleague had recommended me for consideration for this position after a number of interviews I was offered the job and the opportunity to assist in making this unique school a more diverse school environment (children and teachers). It turned out to be a great challenge and emerged as one of the happiest professional experience of my career. Life offers many "twists and turns" and when it falls into a proper place, it is just wonderful. I spent ten magnificent years at a school that reflected the best of what education can be. There were many issues to resolve but none that couldn't be solved professionally. I have many fond memories of my school experiences but this one was very special.

During my final year at Hunter I met with a number of board members from the Marin Country and Day School (a private school in California) who were visiting that day to learn more about the gifted program at Hunter. As the director I met with groups of visitors every week to share information about the school. At the conclusion of this meeting one of Marin's board members asked me if I might be interested in applying for the Headmaster's position which became available at their school due to a recent retirement. This is a private school very similar to your Brentwood School and is also located in California. The opportunity sounded interesting and arrangements were made to fly your grandmother and me to visit the school. It turned out to be a very inviting and exciting opportunity. When we returned to NYC the following week I again spoke before another group of educators (public and private) about the need to provide an enriching and challenging program for children who were identified as gifted and talented. At the conclusion of this meeting a gentleman who described himself as the Headmaster of the Dalton School (a prestigious school in Manhattan) approached me with the possibility of being considered for an administrative position at this private school. He was aware that I had just returned from Marin County. I met with the representatives from Dalton and was overwhelmed with the proposal they presented. I took a long time considering this huge change in direction and finally made the decision to move into the private school world. Going from a public school environment to a private school establishment was a huge adjustment and changed my professional life completely. Economically it secured my future. For someone who started with a salary of $8,000 per year as a beginning teacher to be elevated to this level was well beyond my expectations. At the age of 55 years, I embarked on a new direction in my life. The Dalton school had all the services, teachers, special personnel, small class sizes (12-15 children per class) two full time teachers in each room, a beautiful school building and just about everything that would make a school a rich institution of learning. It was an outstanding world and truthfully was one that should be enjoyed by all children. Having been exposed to private and public educational programs has made me acutely aware of the great gap that exists among people in our democratic society. As a young person who lived on a social security check of $400 per month to support my brothers (ages 19 and 7) after our parents died, I can fully appreciate this discrepancy (difference).

My nine years at Dalton were ideal and challenging, intellectually and emotionally. A very involved parent body that included many families of means and public recognition were an integral part of this institution. Lots of novice and theatrical personalities (ie. Dustin Hoffman, Diana Ross, Woody Allen, Sting, Lenny Kravitz, etc.) walked in and out of the building on a regular basis after visits to their children's classrooms. It was an interesting and glamorous environment. I am please to let you know that Donald Trump applied for admission for his oldest son and he was rejected. I remember that with great satisfaction.

The final year of my tenure at the school included an incident that made it impossible to continue on at Dalton. An event involving a group of boys in the sixth grade who foolishly started a fire in a bathroom by lighting a match to a roll of toilet tissue in what was a regrettable act of lack of discipline and respect for the school. They were caught by some staff members and reprimanded. One of the boys was an Afro-American youngster who attended the school on a full academic scholarship. He was a brilliant student and gifted musician and someone I had grown to be very fond of. The school authorities made a decision to expel this boy from school while the other two boys (who were white) and were equally involved in this misguided act were reprimanded and allowed to remain as students at the school. I requested the opportunity to speak on behalf of the boy before a committee of school personnel and parents. I sincerely felt that what was done was incredibly unfair and illegal. It was a heated meeting and the final outcome did not change the original decision. I was instrumental in getting the boy relocated to another school and I am pleased to report that he graduated, went to college and became an accomplished musician. I have since lost contact with his mother (family) but I trust he is well.

As a result of this situation I was notified that because I was not a "team player". I would not be issued a contract for the coming year. I did initiate a lawsuit against the school and after a number of overwhelming support of the parent body and the school, sought to seek an amiable (suitable) solution to this problem. The outcome resulted in my being offered a position at Bank St. College to supervise a program that was being created to help prepare minority groups (mostly black women) for administrative positions (assistant principals) for the NYC Board of Education. I was sorry to leave the Dalton school in such a fashion but there are occasions in life when you must address the unfairness of issues that are unjust to others and stand firm on your convictions as a caring person. I hope that you can grow to appreciate that concept.

I thoroughly enjoyed my assignment at Bank St. College. It was a different experience for me in that all my contacts were with the Afro-American women interns who aspired to become school administrators. I did visit a large number of schools observing themat work but I had little contact with children and I missed that experience, one that had been part of me for my entire career. My main job was to monitor the progress of each intern. Eight of fifteen women became assistant principals in NYC Board of Education and the remaining candidates required another year or two to qualify for future assignments. It was a great, rewarding year for me but truthfully I missed the ambiance (environment) of a school filled with teachers and loving children and longed to return to a school of my own.

I saw an advertisement in the NY Times submitted by Columbia Grammar and Prep School seeking the services of a head of school and I decided to apply. Everything went well in this interview except for the concern that I was in my sixties (62 to be exact) and the question about how long I would want to stay on at the school was broached (introduced). I said that a period of

3-5 years was likely my horizon and we reached a formal agreement. The fact that I stayed on in that position for almost 20 years was an indication of how much I enjoyed helping rebuild one of the oldest private schools in the country (founded in 1764) into a respected and significant educational institution once again. We "grew" (built) the school from a school population of 500 pupils to its present level of 1200 students during the years I was part of the school's organization. It was done incrementally (year by year) by increasing the number of classes in the Lower School (Grammar School) and gradually enlarging the Prep School (high School) over the years. It changed from a sweet little school on the Westside of Manhattan into a formidable large scale operation and I was pleased to have played a role in that process and, might I add, that much of the credit for the school's growth and development should be extended to the wonderful mixture of dedicated and sincere teachers who worked diligently every day to make the school a true learning environment and a warm place to teach, to learn and to grow within.

At the age of 82 I recognized that it became time for me to leave. The changing politics of the school, the new direction it was taking and philosophical differences I personally felt were unprofessional and misguided. In addition, a very generous retirement package made my choice to leave easy. I left with the love and affection of the children, their parents and a dedicated staff to enter the world of retirement. It was a great, long career and I loved almost every minute of it. I have some regrets but then again, no one is perfect. I carry lots of fond memories with me and they are a constant reminder of how blessed I was to have selected education as my life's work.

I wish you the same good fortune.

Love,
Papa
November 25, 2015

P.S Please excuse the length of this letter. It is difficult to condense 60 plus years into a few pages.

P.S. P.S In addition to what I included in this long letter I am going to present a list of part time positions I held in my field (all part-time and in the evenings) and a list of credentials I achieved while working full time. I was very busy growing up.

1 Bachelor of Science Degree at NYU–The tuition was $7 per credit and during my freshman, sophomore and junior years I worked as a waiter in a hotel in the Catskill Mountains. I made approximately $2,000 per summer which covered my tuition and expenses. My parents died during my scholarship for my last (senior) year.

2 Master of Arts, Brooklyn College– This was a totally free program and part of a Teacher Education Program sponsored by the city of New York.

3 Doctorate of Education, Fordham University– It took me ten years to get this degree (evenings and summers). As a principal, I was assigned interns who were seeking to become assistant principals in the NYC system. I was awarded a free 3-point credit to take courses at Fordham. Since I was able to provide for 15 interns over the years, my tuition for my degree became minimal. It was a long process but well worth it.

4 Teaching on the College Level– Brooklyn College, Educational Psychology/Kingsborough Community College, Workshop for Teacher Aides/Hunter College, Educational Methods and Psychology/Bank St. College, Workshop for Prospective Supervisor Interns and New York City Board of Education, conducted interviews and license examinations for prospective candidates.

Dear Papa,

Thank you for sharing your feelings with me. I was very glad to find out more about you. I was surprised you opened up so much because you can sometimes be like a closed book with a lock. The lock is sometimes opened by my mom and others, but then it is closed again. I enjoyed the submerged submarine quote. I think it is true a lot of the time, and I thought it was funny. You don't normally include funny stuff in your letters because they are normally serious. I thought that saying "Let us begin" was very formal, and an unusual way to start a conversation. Also, you put a lot of emotion into this letter. I did not expect this topic to come up, so it was a pleasant surprise.

Normally when I ask questions to people, they give me short answers with minimal detail. I feel like nobody talks openly to me because I am a kid.

It surprised me because nobody has opened up to me this much in my life. Normally when I ask questions to people, they give me short answers with minimal detail. I feel like nobody talks openly to me because I am a kid. Most kids have that feeling, like they want to shout, "Stop treating me like a kid!" (Even though they are a kid.) I feel like I'm at a high maturity level and can be exposed to new ideas and topics. I sometimes get peeved that I don't hear what's going on. Maybe I could help in a situation that is tough or difficult.

My parents sometimes tell me more mature content, but I feel like they don't always tell me the whole truth. They aren't lying but they aren't telling the full truth. Maybe this happens because

27

it actually is too mature for me. An example is my mom's work. She sometimes works with people that aren't the nicest. She tells me about her day at work and if some people were rude or nice to her, but sometimes I think she does not tell me everything. I understand if she thinks something is too mature for me or if she wants to keep it private, but I would like to know what's going on in her life. Maybe my opinion could help her solve a problem.

Do certain people help you solve any problems? Do you have a best friend (other than nana)? In your letter, you said you had many friends who are women. What are their names? How did you meet them? What stories do u have about them? What impact did they have on your life? Did you know any of these women when your parents died? Did they comfort you?
Speaking of your parents, you went to temple for two years after they passed. Though I am not very religious, I know that 2 years of temple day and night is a lot. Did you ever get bored of it? If so, did you remind yourself that this was for your parents?

You got a job as an usher when you were 18. Was this experience something that you remember? What impact did this job have on you? Did it make you think about what you wanted to be during your career? When I get older I want to work with kids. Maybe teaching them basketball, hanging out with them, or help them in school.

Thank you very much for giving me insight on your life and feelings. It has helped me get a better understanding about you as a person. Thank you for all the amazing life lessons you have taught me. They will be very useful someday.

Love,
Jaden

P.S. You also talked about a women gene implanted in everyone.

What woman gene are you talking about? Are you referring to different stereotypes between men and women? There are different stereotypes about women being more sensitive or being very easy to share your feelings with (compared to men). But some men are more sensitive than some women. Sometimes stereotypes aren't true. Men and women act differently depending on their personality. Is "the gene" a typical stereotype or is it something else?

❧

Dear Jaden,

I was very impressed with your recent letter regarding your impressions of the "long letter." I wrote to you a few weeks ago, your writings reveal a lot of insight on your part plus the evidence of a good sense of humor. It may be difficult for you to appreciate but I also have been told that I have a good sense of humor and I regret that you haven't been able to appreciate that part of me thus far in the letters and experiences we have shared.

I will try in the future to be less pedantic (teacher-like) in my writings to you and I will attempt to make a sincere effort in the future to "lighten up" and inject some humor into the letters we share. However, keep in mind that my 87 year old sense of humor might be different from your 12 year old outlook on life and view about what represents "funny."

I am pleased that you enjoyed my little story about the comparison of a submerged submarine to my social interactions with people. That small tidbit is a reflection of my sense of humor and I promise to share more of it with you in the future. Your thoughts and evaluations of our written communications has great merit. Please remember that the first 50 letters I wrote you were responded to by brief verbal comments that you made by telephone and now that the tide has turned to the point where we are writing to each other on a regular basis we have become truly engage in our conversations.

Your surprise about the amount of emotion I revealed in my last few letters was remarkably insightful on your part and I am pleased that you were able to appreciate this change of direction. It is my intention for you to get to know me better not only as your grandfather but also as a feeling and compassionate person. Your desire to have adult (your parents, etc.) to stop treating you as a kid (your words) and to allow you to communicate with adults on a more mature and realistic level is very admirable.

However, it must also be appreciated on your part that when you enter into this form of relationship you must do so with the ability to listen and respect the differences in the points of views and opinions that exist between you and your adult family and friends. I feel confident that your parents would love to reach out to you and engage in deeper and move meaningful discussions however, you must grow to display behavior and understand beyond your years to allow them to have the confidence to include you in the same adult exchanges. Your opinions and thoughts will always be respected as you grow developmentally. You have already exhibited a demeanor (behavior) that is much more mature than your age and continued growth on your part as a Pre-adolescent and adolescent will gain you the respect you deserve and desire. Your parents are waiting patiently to involve you in all of the facets (parts) of your family life. It is up to you to exhibit your readiness for such a responsibility and yes, your carefully developed opinions would be welcomed.

Now allow me to time to address the other questions you posed in your letter. Regarding the "many women in my life" which you mentioned and questioned me about. I believe that I indicated in my letter to you that 60-70 years ago women were basically limited to three fields of endeavors. They could become teachers, nurses, secretaries or get married and care for their children. We have come a long way in that regard but in those days my chosen field of education was female dominated. As a young teacher in my twenties I taught at a school that included many older white – haired teachers (like your old grandfather is today). They were very kind to me and adopted me as their long lost son. I enjoyed those days and studied hard to become a school administrator. The rest of my career I worked with hundreds of female teachers and the female "gene" I referred to is the one devoted to nurturing and caring for children and people which appears to be part of the DNA of almost every woman. I adopted this "gene trait" and used it well during my tenure which covered 60 years.

You were right about the time I spent going to synagogue (temple) every morning and evening to repeat the mourners' (Kaddish) prayer for a two year period on behalf of my parents. It was a difficult experience for me to endure but I felt it was a commitment I had to fulfill on behalf of my parents.

Finally, I did work as an usher in the local movie house in my neighborhood during the time I was a high school student. My parents were ill and I needed to assist my family financially. I enjoyed seeing all the movies for free. My only problem was that each film played at the theater for an entire week. It became boring at times.

I hope you enjoyed this letter and I await your response to the letter about "The state of Politics in the USA. That I mailed to you previously.

Stay well and try to locate that "female gene" in your inner self. It is a worthwhile discovery.

Love,
Papa & Nana
February 10, 2016

Dear Jaden,

Your mom and dad confided (told me) the other day that since you returned from Florida back to California that they noticed a great many positive changes in your demeanor (behavior) and overall manner in your dealings with all the people who surround you (family and friends). When you were in Florida I couldn't help but notice how well you related with your new cousins (Adam's daughters) and the new environment (Florida) that you were part of for a few days.

There were lots of good examples of the growth in maturity that you displayed during your visit that make all of us proud of you. The items that stood out as exemplary (excellent) were as follows. Your mature and involved presence at each meal we had together (you really are good company), your ability to integrate (join) into a basketball game with older boys and in the swimming area with lots of people and your skill to assert yourself in positive ways when speaking to all different kinds of people. On the whole, your ability to accept all the events of the holiday season in an open and receptive fashion and most importantly, to be able to do this without any display of moodiness or discomfort was a joy to observe. Great job!!! You are really growing up and learning how to enjoy all people for the many positives they bring to your life.

Keep in mind that when someone gets "moody" (acts in an irritable or upset way) it usually means that this person is upset with himself or lacks the skills to express himself appropriately. You are most fortunate because you are very articulate (speak well) and you respect the feelings of others. Your moods are usually positive and supportive. You are also surrounded with love from your family and friends. In addition, you have developed a keen sense of humor which helps to defuse (stop) most disputes and difficult events.

Allow me to encourage you to use those previously mentioned positive techniques to help others through their periods of moodiness or unpleasantness and recognize that there will be some "rare" occasions when you might need to internalize (look within) for the needed support when you feel uneasy and/or upset about an issue (problem) you are facing. All thinking humans go through that process.

Maintain your very appealing approach to life that obviously is a part of who you are as a person and know that we are all proud of the direction in which you are moving.

Love,
Papa & Nana
January 19, 2015

MEANING OF FEAR

Dear Jaden,

Now that the holiday Halloween is almost upon us, I thought it might be a good idea to write you about how to deal with "fearful" situation whether they be real or artificial as presented during Halloween. Fear is something we all face as we grow and how secure you are as a person will best determine how successful you will be in dealing with this emotion. What I am trying to say is that it is appropriate for you to see some situations as being upsetting or dangerous and to respond accordingly. Fear is a "state of mind" and the more you control your feelings (anger, upset or real concern) the more likely it will be that you will meet the challenge with success.

As a boy, as a man, as a parent and as a teacher I have always had a distaste for the holiday–Halloween–because I have always felt that it emphasized feelings and actions that promote fear and discomfort, particularly among children. I am hopeful that you accept this "silly" celebration as a "make believe" adventure into the world of ghosts, goblins and freaky characters which should be addressed as pure fun and meaningless. I would rather you spend your time in other kinds of worthwhile activities that enhance your life instead of engaging in the commercial world of Halloween. I guess that it is best to just enjoy this "silly" day for the fun it might provide and not take it too seriously.

Now, I would like to address the term "fear" and the role it plays in your life. Everyone faces this feeling in his life and it is really fine to be afraid of something or someone who might be a challenge to you. In those cases, you need to call upon your inner strengths to deal with whatever you face. You possess a good sense of who you are and you have a strong passion to appreciate what is wrong and what is right. In challenging situations, I suggest that you work hard to control your emotions, speak softly but directly to the situation you are facing and maintain your dignity at all times. Most fearful situations turn out to be less frightening and disturbing as time passes. Maintain a strong presence even though you might be scared, and diminish the "crises" you are facing, and always keep in mind that no matter what happens you will always have the support of your family and loved ones and that should strengthen your resolve.

We all face difficult moments in our lives. How you handle these challenging moments will be determined by what and how you feel about yourself. I have no doubt that you will meet these issues with great success. The key will be embedded in you self-concept. I trust and know that your solid upbringing and the love you received in your formative years will hold you in good stead.

> Good Luck and Blessings.
> Love,
> Papa & Nana
> October 22, 2014

Dear Jaden,

I was pleased to hear that you enjoyed an overnight experience with your friends recently and that you are looking forward to going to a summer camp away from home after the school year ends in June. Those are very grown up moves and while I don't look forward to your growing up too quickly, it is rewarding to learn that you are moving in a positive way toward maturity. It is often difficult to adjust to changes in one's life but with proper guidance from your parents and mature growth on your part the transitional periods in your life will become smoother, less challenging and easily achievable as you grow to maturity.

One of the key decisions one must make in his (or her) life is choosing a profession (job opportunity) when reaching the exalted position of adulthood. You are a long way from there but what you are doing in your young and growing years will help determine what path you will follow in selecting a future profession (occupation) when you reach adulthood. Lots of what you are occupied with at school and through your outside interests and experiences will aid you in making a decision in this important portion of your future life.

I would like to devote the balance of this letter to sharing some of my experiences in the decision I made as a developing person in the hope and expectation that you will utilize your preteen and coming teenage years to start thinking of what you would like to do with your adult life and what contributions you might be able to make for the welfare of others including family, friends and society, in general. Remember, you have received many "gifts" from your parents, such as your intelligence, personality, physical appearance, interests and a host of many positive traits and characteristics plus the inclusion of a few that need to be developed and refined since none of us are perfect human beings (except for your mother and father). You are fortunate to have such a strong foundation to build upon.

When I was a boy I always enjoyed going to school. I liked learning but more importantly I cherished the friendships, sporting activities and the security of being in an environment that was supportive and accepting. Because I loved sports and enjoyed success in this area, I dreamed of becoming a major league baseball player when I grew up. This dream changed when I realized that very few people reached that goal and that I needed to think of a profession that would meet my needs as an adult. I went to college to study to become a teacher (which would also allow me to coach children in various sports) and it turned out to be a perfect fit for me.

In my last year at college my parents unfortunately got sick and passed away. I received my degree from college after a very difficult period of time and got a job as a teacher in an inner-city school in Brooklyn. I had a difficult time at first since very little can prepare you for a teaching position in a classroom of 40 children with diverse abilities and personalities. My entire class was comprised of Afro-American children

All I ask of you is that you make a decision that will fulfill your potential and meet your needs as a caring and feeling person.

and while I couldn't truly understand and appreciate their circumstances, they accepted me as their teacher (mentor) and friend and I grew to love them as my pupils and as members of my family. It became very apparent that I had made the right decision about my chosen profession. I am hopeful that you will feel the same love in your life when you make your decision about your field of work.

I must have been totally enamored (in love) with my work otherwise I wouldn't have lasted over sixty (60) years as an educator. I would truly want you to have the opportunity to feel the same enthusiasm for the work you choose to follow. Making great amounts of money should not be the main goal in your life. I do want you to be comfortable and secure in whatever you decide will be your life's work, however, it is just as important to have a positive impact on as many lives as you can during your time on earth and that your legacy (contribution) should be acknowledged through your dealings in every facet (part) of your life with people who have shared a piece of your existence (stay) on earth.

You have a long way to go before any decision about what you will be doing as an adult in the world of work. All I ask of you is that you make a decision that will fulfill your potential and meet your needs as a caring and feeling person.

Best of luck!!!!

Love,
Papa & Nana
May 10, 2014

RELIGIOUS BELIEFS

Dear Jaden,

I thought that this might be a good time to broach (introduce) my thoughts to you about the concept of religion and to include the significance of the "bar mitzvah" ritual in the life of a boy who is turning into the beginning of manhood as he enters his 13th year as a member of the Jewish faith. I never considered myself to be religious as defined as a practicing active Jew by attending the synagogue and praying on a regular basis. However, I do consider myself religious in that I live a relatively good and wholesome life and follow the parameters (boundaries) of what would be considered appropriate in the teachings of the Bible and the followers of the Jewish faith. I did not come from a religious family, but it was one that believed in God, nevertheless. I was bar mitzvahed at 13 years of age and I did go to a Sunday hebrew school for a period of time.

On a personal note, as I grew up and read and learned about ancient history and past history I did question and become somewhat distressed by the many religious wars and tragic events that took place in the name of God. Religious beliefs and misinterpretations of what they really represent have been used for evil purposes in the past, and even today we see its abuses in the Middle-East where some vile people (Isis, etc.) us their false version of the Muslim religion to subjugate (control) and destroy people. I needed to learn to keep in mind (as I hope you will to) that it is not the religion or the wonderful teachings it espouses (to express support) but the depravity and ill will that some people use to help them achieve horrible results in their false interpretation of religious beliefs. What I have learned over the years is that the different religions that people follow (i.e. Christian, Jewish, Muslim, Mormon, etc.) are primarily good and offer solace and peace to all people, but unfortunately it can also be used by others who are deceitful, ignorant and vicious, for evil purposes as they interpret the religious beliefs to meet their own depraved and ugly needs.

...I always felt that someone or something was overlooking my family, that many wonderful things took place that allowed us to grow, develop and even prosper.

When I reached the age of 21 I had to face an awakening when both my parents died (one year after the other) and left me and my brothers to fend on our own. I lost faith in God because I couldn't believe that any feeling or worthwhile God would take away parents from their children at such an early stage. My despair and anger became greater when I was told that according to the Jewish faith that, as the oldest son, it was my responsibility to attend every morning and evening the synagogue service to recite

38

the mourner's prayer on their behalf and this covered a period of almost two years. It was there that I truly learned to cry and mourn for my parents. I lost faith in religion and God at that time. Becoming a "man" during my bar mitzvah didn't prepare me for this.

On a positive note, as the years went by I always felt that someone or something was overlooking my family, that many wonderful things took place that allowed us to grow, develop and even prosper. While things were difficult and my feelings about God where confused, it became important for me (and you as well) to realize that what matters in life is what your parents provided for you (personally, spiritually and emotionally) while you grow as a person and that will determine who you are as a functioning adult.

Now, let me try to bring you to an understanding and appreciation about why you should be looking forward to your bar mitzvah. I don't expect you to become a very religious and observant Jew. I would however, like you to know that you were born to a Jewish family and as such the bar mitzvah ritual is one you should embrace and enjoy. It is a relatively simple procedure and it would bring joy to your family. What road you follow after that is your choice. On a practical note, when you reach the 7th grade you will be invited and will attend many bar mitzvahs and bat mitzvahs and the sharing to that experience should be meaningful.

The decision is yours and your parents'. I have tried to share a little history with you and your parents to assist you in your thinking about this issue.

Love,
Papa & Nana
March 12, 2015

Dear Jaden,

Today we are going to discuss why learning to take a risk at certain times in your life can provide you with a meaningful and worthwhile learning experience. One which will enhance (improve) you as a growing and developing young man. We all want to be safe and feel secure in what we are doing whether it be at school, at work, at a gathering or at any other occasion when one has to make a decision that will have an impact on others. This is because we are part of a world in which we play, work, socialize and function as contributing and caring persons.

"Taking a risk" is no easy task. The possibility of failure or offending people you know and care for might be the outcome of the risk you take if it ends poorly. It does however require some fortitude (strength) and faith in oneself to go against the will of those you know and might care for. Most of your life will be devoted to being a member of a community (family, friends, co-workers, etc.) and being part of such a group will mean that in the majority of situations you will be in agreement with the boundaries that encompasses (surrounds) this group. You would also usually conduct yourself as a supporting, positive and engaged force within your selected group. However, there may come a time when you choose to challenge or deviate (stray) from the wishes and desires of the other for a rationale (reason) that is unique to you and your sense of self-control.

Allow me to present a few simple examples of what I mean about "taking a risk" that might be more beneficial to you in the process of your development as an independent, thinking adult. Let's conjecture (imagine) that as a teenager you become involved with a group of friends who choose to smoke cigarettes or experiment with drugs. They urge you to do the same and if you refuse they intend to ostracize (remove) you from the group and forgo your friendship. You could join them as a smoker or take a risk of losing their friendship. That is a risk worth taking. Other similar opportunities might include befriending a boy or

40

girl who the majority of your friends reject because of his (her) race, family background or physical appearance and you choose to ignore their actions. There will be times when you will have to assert yourself because you feel strongly about some issue that touches you emotionally as a feeling person. To go against the will of others and to fight for something you feel strongly about takes strength of character and will, in the end, be valued. This will gain you respect from your friends and even from those who disagree with you because you have emerged as someone with a "soul" who is open to change and receptive to all kinds of people.

You can say no or take a different road from others as long as you believe in yourself and in the rights of others to hold different points of view and lifestyles. No two people are the same (including identical twins) and you should strive to take chances if you feel strongly about something and allow yourself to learn from the "risks" you take whether they be positive or negative. The key to taking a chance or deviating (moving) from the straight and narrow is your self-confidence. There is nothing wrong in making a mistake. Not following through on what you feel might be a worthwhile effort would be unfortunate. There were a number of events in my life, for example, the Civil Rights movement, School Integration, Gay Rights and many educational issues that I personally took risks with during my career. Some I won and some I lost, but all of them shaped my life and provided me with satisfaction and good feeling. You don't have to win every battle. Some "risks" take long to materialize but each experience is full of growth and opportunity for someone like you.

I wish you well in meeting the challenges you face in "growing up".

Love,
Papa & Nana
July 24, 2014

Dear Jaden,

    I thought it would be a great idea to take time to address the issue of "separation" (time away from your parents) now that you have reached the ripe "old age" of eleven. As you grow to maturity, you will become aware that you will be spending less and less time with your parents as you develop interests, friendships and a world of activities that are exciting and time consuming. When you were a baby and toddler, all of your time and needs were provided for by your parents. As a result of this, the bond that you developed with your mother and farther became a powerful force in your life. This is the foundation that was created and it will remain firm and supportive during the balance of your life on earth. It will be the core (essence) of your being forever.

Growing up is not easy and you should feel blessed to have your caring, loving family to support you through that process.

    When you started school, the experience of being away from your parents for the good part of the day was to be the first "separation" you had to face. You did nicely because you trusted them and you enjoyed the attractive, challenging school environment. You have now entered into your middle school years and you have engaged in other similar activities such as camp, sleepovers, etc. that also separate you from them for periods of time. You have, in addition, spent time with friends, playing a variety of sports and just socializing with large numbers of boys and girls that you have cultivated when you were not with your parents. All of that is very healthy and age appropriate and are important factors (parts) in allowing you to become an independent, confident, thinking person as you grow toward adulthood. Growing up is not easy and you should feel blessed to have your caring, loving family to support you through that process. You are now facing a problem that is no longer unique since the family organization (structure) of our time has changed considerably in the past few years. At one time, not that many years ago, it was one parent who was employed (usually the father) who worked full time and there was one parent (usually the mother) at home to provide for the needs of the child or children on a full time basis. Today, we have many families where both parents work during the day and their children are provided for by caregivers and other members of the extended family.

I truly recognize that you miss your parents when you are away from them during the day. They are both busy doing some very very important work to provide for others and themselves. All people (including your parents) need to feel that they are contributing something for the welfare of others while they are fortunate to be making a good living that will enhance their lives and their family. Keep in mind, that at all times one of your parents is available to be there for you on a moment's notice on any day you might need them (i.e. illness, accident, etc.) and in your case, your father's flying schedule is such that he's home many days during the week when most fathers are not.

It is extremely sweet that you miss your dad when he goes off to work. You have a close relationship with him and as a result, it is really important that the time you spend together remain special. You are extremely fortunate because you also have the same relationship with your mother. You are one "lucky" fellow and I implore (beg) you to make certain that the time you spend with one or the other not be squandered (wasted) but cherished. It really doesn't depend upon how much time you have with them, but more importantly, how well spent was the time you shared.

Now, allow me to digress (change the topic) and share some personal additional thoughts I have about how people like you should spend their "free" time. On a personal note, I have always enjoyed the few moments that I had to myself on any given day. Being alone allows you the opportunity to get to know yourself better. I like to read by myself and think thoughts that are of concern to me. You really can converse (talk) to yourself (not aloud but inwardly) in your mind and you would be amazed how many good answers you get to the questions that are posed (presented).

I also like to swim alone and walk around town (the city) by myself and just think and enjoy the scenery. Working in the garden (Sag Harbor) is another solitary thing I like to do and the feedback you get from the plants is incredibly rewarding. I share this with you not to have you think how strange your grandfather is but in the hope that you will discover the many blessings and opportunities afforded (provided) to you during your life. It is a thought you might consider or at least talk to yourself about.

Love,
Papa & Nana
July 24, 2015

SHORTCUTS

Dear Jaden,

I just read through your recent repot card and I am very proud of how well you are doing at school. It is apparent that your teachers like you as a person and are impressed with you as a student, Congratulations on a job well done.

I did however, notice that while you are a good writer and express yourself beautifully, your teachers felt that on occasion, in responding to written questions and assignments, you sometimes use a "shortcut" approach to answering your written questions. They recognize that you know the material well but that you don't embellish (enlarge) your answers to the point where you have given a completely thorough response to the question being posed.

Since it is apparent that you do have the knowledge and intelligence to be outstanding in this area of learning, I would like to recommend a few strategies that you might want to follow to help you elaborate and add more "meat" or completeness to your answers.

Allow me to illustrate with an example. Let's say that your social studies teacher gives you a homework assignment that includes the question "What achievement did Christopher Columbus accomplish as a result of his exploration trip to the new world called America?" After reading the question carefully, the first thing you need to do is write, in an outline from, a few words about each of the achievements that he accomplished and list them on a piece of scrap paper (not the paper you are submitting to your teacher).

Some of the brief notes might include "he proved that the world wasn't flat", "discovered America", "found a new world rich in natural resources", "opened exploration opportunities for others", "made Spain a rich and leading country in the world at that time", etc. you could list more items on your own, but let's stop there for now. Having completed the list you are now ready to write the answer to your homework assignment. By the way, this list will take very little of your time but most importantly it makes the final writing easier.

The next procedure is to go back to your original question and use it as part of your answer. For example, the first statement in your response should read, "Columbus made many achievements as a result of his exploration of the new world." Go back and look at your list of his achievements, and write them in single, whole sentences including a subject and predicate such as, "He discovered a new world called America," "His long voyage proved that the world was not flat," and you continue on to the next item, writing full sentences about each accomplishment which you had recorded earlier in outline form.

When you have finished writing the entire list you will have a complete and excellent answer to the question. It is really an easy process and your teachers will love your complete and thoughtful answers.

This is just a small technique that will help make you be a better organized and competent student and it will reflect positively in your school achievement. Try it!!! It worked for me and hopefully you will enjoy the same success.

Looking forward to seeing you during the holidays.

Again, Congratulations on your excellent report card!!

Love,
Papa & Nana
December 12, 2014

to what I am writing about in
to explain this relationship.
any game being played whev
ants, it usually means that c
t win and one must lose. The cov
control the sport being played
follow. The major factors tha
game (sport) are the rules and
mine the boundaries of the spor
in life, there are occasions wh
outcome as a result of your ef
ame or action or activity that pv
isfaction. However, there will b
ose in a sporting event which
pain" and upset. Life operates t
up and engage in many activit
people to disagree with you an
onflict" that puts you and them.
e a game, you will win the av
ing upon how well you develop
t of view as opposed to your
the dispute. In most cases,

CHAPTER 2

The Inner Self

Letters on Emotions and How to Navigate Feelings

Dear Jaden,

Please forgive me for not writing sooner. I have been very busy with my garden and house in Sag Harbor and I am happy to say that everything is growing and thriving and is awaiting a visit from you.

Today, I thought it would be a good idea to share some of my thoughts with you about the feeling of "anger" and how to deal with this emotion since it is a force that all of us face at some point in our lives. It is very important that you learn to appreciate how to best deal with the impact this can have on you and the people who are part of your environment.

We all get upset or angered with events and/or people who hurt or abuse our feelings and sense of security. It is absolutely vital that you learn how to react to a hurtful situation without losing your sense of identity and self-value. The one thing you must always keep in mind is that you must strive not to lose your own self-dignity by responding in anger or with abusive language or physical action to the person(s) directing this awful behavior toward you. You have every reason and right to be upset (angered) but it is important for your self-worth to learn how to deal with all negative situations in a calm, self-assured manner to help diffuse (lessen) the explosiveness of any conflict you might be facing.

Expressions of anger are usually short-lived and often embarrassing for the aggressor and by maintaining your own "cool" you will often lessen the feeling for the need for conflict. You are not being a "coward" when you recognize the need to remove yourself from an untenable situation and attempt to create a more suitable opportunity to communicate in normal voice tones to address issues that might be controversial or threatening to the people involved in the dispute.

Unfortunately, there will be some hostility and anger in your life regardless of how you seek to avoid it. Choose your friends and colleagues wisely and look for individuals who share the same values and beliefs that you possess. Life is full of many wonderful, happy experiences and it is further enhanced when you surround yourself with people you respect and love.

You have every right to be angry or upset at times. It is how you deal with this anger, and the strengths you develop as a functioning person, that will make the difference in your life.

Good luck with your voyage!

Love,
Papa & Nana
June 10, 2014

BEING BORED

Dear Jaden,

Today I am going to write you about one of my favorite topics that I used to discuss with many of the boys and girls I worked with at the schools where I taught and administered. Being "bored" was a common term used by children when they felt dissatisfied (unhappy) with their day at school. There are many activities that take place during the day (in and out of school) that one might find unappealing or lacking in excitement or interest which you and other nine-year-olds would label as "boring." In the world where you are growing up, and enjoying as an active participant, an environment that strives for the instant gratification and immediate response has been created.

This means that very little thinking is required since all you have to do is press a button or a switch as you do in computer games and Wi-Fi activities. This approach requires little thinking or planning on your part, but it does provide you with immediate action and involvement. I am not certain that your brain (intellect) is gaining much from these activities but they are lots of fun.

51

Now, let's look at the word "boring". The dictionary meaning is : "To become tired, repetitious or dull." What does that mean to us as people? Boring can sometimes mean that you are not happy or pleased with yourself or your surroundings. A person is usually not bored when he or she has a good sense of self and enjoys thinking on his (her) own.

Thomas Edison (inventor), Jonas Salk (medicine) and many other accomplished people spent great amounts of time and energy thinking and exploring many areas of interest that appealed to their intellectual curiosity and much of their work would be identified as tedious, time consuming and boring. Look at what they accomplished. Being bored is truly a state of mind and if you are a real learner, possessing an open mind you will be able to find value in whatever task or problem you are seeking to solve.

Being "bored" is often an excuse for being unprepared or unwilling to extend oneself because of a lazy attitude or a fear of failure. You must remember that failure can also be a learning tool. You learn much from your mistakes and they usually make you a better and wiser person.

Being "bored" can also be looked upon as a challenge. People who are strong in mind and purpose often fight through this feeling and as a result, become more complete and successful as contributing members of our society. There is nothing wrong about feeling "bored" on occasion. The key is to take the opportunity and the time to stretch yourself by encouraging your imagination and intelligence to be creative in using the time you face in these "boring" moments in a productive and worthwhile manner. An occasional "day dream" or happy thought can often get you started.

Time on earth is limited for all of us. Use it well and enjoy the opportunities that are exciting and memorable, but don't forget the dull periods. They have value as well.

Love,
Papa & Nana
December 8, 2013

Dear Jaden,

    Today I would like to introduce you to a new vocabulary word. It is called "empathy". The dictionary definition of this word is: "The ability to understand and respect the feelings of others." It is a beautiful word and it is important that you grow to understand its full meaning and grow to allow this feeling of "empathy" to engulf (surround) your entire being and guide you in your dealings and relationships with the many different kinds of people who will come and go during your life on earth.

    There will be some people you will establish relationships with who face unusually difficult circumstances in their lives. People who are less fortunate than you and who are burdened with hardships and difficulties that overwhelm them and don't allow them to enjoy and share in the abundance of wonderful experiences that should be made available to all people. I am referring to those who are handicapped (physically & emotionally), the poor and needy who lack shelter, food and the necessities of life due to a loss of jobs, unhealthy family relationships, illness and a host of other reasons that most of us will fortunately escape and will never have to face.

    There are a few individuals in our country who look upon this ever growing group as lazy, unworthy people who are prone (likely) to take advantage of our democratic system of government by abusing the services our country provides for the needy. Now, there might be a few unscrupulous people who do fall into that category but they are few in number and the vast majority of the poor in our country could not exist without some support and services. A simple sense of humanity and an appreciation for the wellbeing of all persons should lead us to a positive understanding in this issue. We are a wealthy country and morally and spiritually we need to be resolved to support and assist each other in time of need. We must be able to emphasize this approach with all people and this can be done in many ways. The numbers of those who are classified as impoverished (poor) continues to grow. There is a need for housing, creating job opportunities, food, education, health facilities and much more to help those among us who are less fortunate.

You are a "lucky" young boy and in all likelihood, you will never need the assistance I mentioned previously. However, this does not preclude (prevent) you from developing into an "empathetic" (feeling) person who respects all people and provides time, energy, love and care for those in need.

At this time I would like to share with you my reasons for feeling so strongly about this issue. I will always remain forever indebted and grateful to our government for the financial support my brothers and I received from social security and the welfare department after our parents died when we were young (ages 21, 20 and 6) and unable to support ourselves. Without that assistance we would never have been able to survive. We were provided with the needed means which allowed each of us to grow and achieve success and happiness in our lives.

I encourage you to use your mother as a role model and guide in learning how to help others. Her position as a professional fundraiser to help provide goods and services for the poor and needy is extremely noteworthy and worth emulating (imitating). I would like you to be able to "feel the pain" of others and to become an understanding and giving person as you grow and developed into manhood. You've made a great start in this direction and I urge you to continue your growth as an understanding, sensitive and loving man. You possess all the ingredients to become a special human being. Stay true to yourself and the world in which you live and share with others.

Love,
Papa & Nana
February 1, 2015

P.S. Please share this letter with some Republican friends & family you may know.

Dear Jaden,

Today I chose to write to you about the feeling of being "stressed". Even during your young life there will be times when you are going to feel stress or "out of sorts" because of some pressure or overwhelming feeling that is harbored (located) in you that reflect events that are not going the way you would like. It is frustrating to feel impotent (weak) when most of the time you truly feel you are on the "top of things" and that life is relatively good and functioning smoothly.

Let us look at how we might be able to face those periods of stress and overcome that limited period of feeling inadequate and unable to deal with the challenges you are facing. First of all, you must recognize that all people get frustrated or stressed at some points in their lives. You are not alone in that regard. What separates those who can't deal with stress and those who are able to counter (fight back) this dreadful feeling is something that is embedded (hidden) in their personalities. It is, however, found within the makeup of those who can, in positive ways work through these moments of difficulty. In my opinion, your strong personality and keen ability to make appropriate adjustments to the challenges you face will help guide you through the turmoils (difficulties) of being stressed.

Most importantly, you have to find faith in yourself to be able to meet whatever the situation might be that is troubling you. This inner strength will help you to recognize the problem and provide you with the understanding that whatever the issue might be that is concerning you and causing stress is one that will eventually pass and not necessarily harm you permanently.

Today's problems are often not that devastating in the months and years that follow. You need to put things in proper perspective (a correct place) and learn that there are "ups and downs" in life and that time is often a healing process. Everyone goes through that in life and those who are more successful in achieving their goals embrace that concept.

Remember you are "entitled" to your moments of stress (feeling overwhelmed). It is how you deal with those times and how you prepare yourself to deal with those moments that will define you as a person. You can prepare yourself for periods of stress by engaging in activities that provide you with moments of self-reflection and calmness. I will share some of the things I do to help me in this regard. I try to have a number of quiet times for myself when I read, write, swim, garden, daydream, rest quietly, walk, talk to myself (internally) and just find some quiet, peaceful things to do that relax me. You can do the same but I would suggest that computer activities don't fall into that category.

Know yourself, your strengths and weaknesses and don't overestimate what others can do for you. If you feel comfortable and at ease with yourself then life's challenges will be met with grace and an understanding that, while there will be many achievements that you will enjoy, the set-backs or losses that you encounter will also make you stronger and more appreciative of who you are and what you have. You are as I have indicated before, "entitled" to your periods of stress. In time, they will make you stronger.

Love,
Papa and Nana
March 22, 2015

Dear Papa,

You have to be a special type of person to be able to manage time and other activities. I feel that when some of my friends get stressed out about doing school work, they don't do their best work. They just try to worry about getting the work done, but they don't think about efficiency. When I get stressed out about something, my mind works very differently than others'. The first thing I think about is prioritizing my work. Then, I try to finish my homework for the week by Monday and Tuesday. I don't like being a last minute type of person. I like getting work done because it keeps me stress free.

That being said, I sometimes get a little nervous before athletic games. When I think about how I will do in games, I get stressed out. In those situations, I tend to do worse than when I don't think about the game. When I start to think about how I will do in an upcoming game, I try to take my mind off it. I fidget and play around with objects to take my mind off of the game. It works because it makes me feel more concentrated about things other than sports.

I also get stressed about bigger and more important things in the world. Terrorism is one of those things. It makes me sad to here on the news that other countries are getting bombed. It isn't necessary to inflict violence on other countries. If anybody watches movies or listens in general, people say "violence is never the answer." The thing that stresses me out is thinking about the USA or other countries getting seriously attacked. In this situation I don't really have a technique for dealing with stress, but I feel better knowing that there is an army of people that will protect our country.

Though I don't have a stress technique for dealing with terrorism, I do have one strategy that is good for other things. Computer games are good ways to deal with stress for many reasons. Computer games stimulate your mind and make you focus on something other than what you are stressing about. And Papa, you watch a lot of TV(mostly the news). Why do you not recommended electronics for relieving stress?

Stress can be an overpowering thing in one's life, but people have to learn to deal with it at some point. Stress may seem dif-

ficult to overcome sometimes, so always keep calm and either develop strategies or use some that you have learned.
Love,
Jaden

P.S. I love the story when you got your whole garden eating by a deer. Also, there was a time when there was a hornet's nest next to your house. You tried to hit it and make it go away but an abundance of hornets came at you and forced you to jump into the pool. I can imagine that you had a lot of stress that day. If this happened to me, I would not be stressed, but be in state of mind like "Why me. Why do bad things happen to good people."

FRUSTRATION

Dear Jaden,

I was pleased to learn about your recent interest in the welfare of the many thousands of veterans who have returned from the battlefields of our recent wars. As you have discovered, there are many who are finding it difficult to adjust to their previous lives. The numerous homeless and "wounded warriors" among our returning veterans present serious issues for our society today. Your desire to work with others to support and assist these forgotten and neglected heroes is a very commendable avenue for you to follow. I wish you great success with the project you are seeking to support, involving the many returning vets who are facing such difficult times. It is a gracious and commendable thought and it should provide you with much satisfaction.

Your efforts to help those worthy young men and women will require lots of effort on your part to accomplish. Please don't get discouraged. Some people use anger to express their inner feelings when they face obstacles that defer (block) their efforts. Expressing your anger allows you to relieve some of the frustration you are feeling but its doesn't solve any problems. One needs to approach and utilize that energy to help meet the difficulties that are being faced to get this program "off the ground".

You will need your positive energy to convince people about the merits of your project. I sincerely believe that this approach will afford you a more satisfying and rewarding experience in achieving your goals. I share this with you because I feel very strongly that frustration (which will always be part of your life) is something we all face and to meet this challenge one must use a positive stance to make the goal achievable and rewarding.

I encourage you to get advice from your parents and the proper authorities who support the worthwhile program you are motivated to provide for our needy veterans. Don't lose faith in your efforts. Learning to support and assist those in need will help to make you a more complete and happier person. Those of us who possess the ability to help those in need and less fortunate should strive to incorporate that concept into our daily lives. The fact that you have reached that conclusion at such an early age makes me proud to be your grandfather.

Please continue to feel the caring and kind sentiments that are becoming an integral part of you and this stage in your life and continue to maintain your love for all people, especially for those less fortunate and in need.

Love,
Papa & Nana
October 17, 2015

Dear Jaden,

Today I would like to share with you the significance of two emotions which will play a major role in your life. They are labelled as "joy" and "sorrow". Both are strong expressions of feelings that all people face during their time on earth. How they deal with these emotions will determine how successful they will be in meeting the challenges that are thrusted upon them on a daily basis.

Let us first look at the feelings of joy and happiness since those emotional responses are more pleasant to describe and share. Happiness is a state of mind. When things are going well and you are enjoying success in your relationships with others, in your work, your school or other outside recreational pursuits, your movement through your regular routines and activities is smooth and rewarding. Those are the times you need to cherish and keep as part of your memory bank because they are so precious and meaningful. If you grow up (which you will) and you are able to share those joyful moments with those who surround you, then your life will be enriched with relationships that will provide you with great happiness. Life is truly wonderful when everything is going well and you are enjoying the love and good feelings of others.

Unfortunately there will always be "bumps along the road" as you grow and develop into manhood. I wish that I could promise you a smooth never-ending road to happiness but that is not the picture for you or anyone else. There will be some sorrow that you will have to endure as you mature. How you handle and accept the occasional sadness in your life will become a determining factor in how well you will function as a contributing member of your family and to those who are part of the world that you inhabit. Sorrow comes into one's life when it is least expected. It can come in the form of a loss (death) in the family, as a mishap or accident that changes one's life or as an end to a friendship or job opportunity or as an event (tragedy) that is beyond your ability to control or change. There are so many things that can happen which can make your inner world appear dismal.

During my lifetime I have had to experience a number of occasions that brought sadness into my life and affected the course of my development. For example, the loss of my parents at an early age, the facing of personal serious illness, the struggles to grow professionally and personally to reach a level of success despite a number of handicaps, both personal and political, the many issues involved in the raising of a family and a host of other challenges and circumstances that needed to be addressed as one goes through the experiences of daily living. While I felt weakened and true anger toward these obstacles, it also occurred to me that after meeting each challenge with some modicum (small amount) of positive movement that my growth as a functioning human being was enhanced. As I have stated before, there is much to learn from adversity (difficulty) and if you face your "sorrows" with inner strength and understanding, then your moments of joy and happiness as a person will make you a better and more complete individual.

I wish I could promise you a lifelong voyage of smooth and unabated sailing, unfortunately, that is impossible, but the manner in which you manage the low and high points during your development into manhood will determine who you will become and how meaningful your life will be. You have lots to support you in your growth to maturity.

Love,
Papa & Nana
April 11, 2015

Dear Jaden,

  I am truly sorry about the recent result of the outcome of your Super Bowl game last week. Your team lost but they played well and came within inches of winning a coveted victory. Sports in many ways are a real reflection of what "life" is all about and I am hoping that you will pay close attention to what I am writing about in this letter as I try to explain this relationship.

  In any game being played where there are two contestants, it usually means that one person or team must win and one must lose. The conditions and rules that control the sport being played are there for both to follow. The major factors that should guide each game (sport) are the rules and regulations that determine the boundaries of the sporting event.

  As in life, there are occasions when you accomplish a favorable outcome as a result of your efforts and you "win" a game or action or activity that provides you with great satisfaction. However, there will be times when you will lose in a sporting event which will cause you some "pain" and upset. Life operates the same way as you grow up and engage in many activities that will cause some people to disagree with you and enter them into a "conflict" that puts you and them on opposing sides. Like a game, you will win the argument or lose it depending upon how well you develop and present your point of view as opposed to your opponent's vision of the dispute. In most cases, it won't matter who won the disagreement, but it will matter how well you presented yourself as a thinking, sensitive person. In sports there is always one winner and one loser and it is extremely important that the losing team learn from the mistakes that they made in that par-

> *In most cases, it won't matter who won the disagreement, but it will matter how well you presented yourself as a thinking, sensitive person.*

ticular game and use that knowledge to become a better team. We all can learn from our mistakes (errors in judgment) and grow to be better at what we do and become. This will be the same philosophy that you will need to adopt to enable you to grow personally, professionally and emotionally. Learning how to lose with dignity is a difficult task for anyone to learn. I am a living example of that need. I hated to lose but I do feel that I have gained much by evaluating how and why I lost (in games and human relationships).

Your team (Seattle Seahawks) lost the Super Bowl despite the fact that they had victory in their hands. Their last play was a good one but it wasn't executed well. They will learn from that experience and will win games in the future with that same play. It hurts to lose, but it is more upsetting not to learn something about how you lost and how you can grow to improve yourself for the next game or coming segment of your life.

Life has many ups and downs. Enjoy the happiness that comes from a successful experience in sports and in growing up. You are fortunate in that most of your experiences in life will be positive. However, what will determine your true worth will be how you respond to the obstacles and difficulties that you have to face as you develop as a person.

Good luck in your voyage to maturity and look forward to a winning season for the Seahawks next year!

Love,
Papa & Nana
July 24, 2014

Dear Jaden,

    My letter for this week will be centered on the meaning of "love" and the part this feeling of emotion will play in your life. There is a book entitled "The Little Prince" (that I hope you will read when you are in high school) which included a beautiful statement that has great meaning and significance. I would like to share it with you. Please read it slowly and spend some time thinking about its meaning. It reads as following, "One sees clearly only with the heart. Anything essential is invisible to the eye." In other words, we need to allow the love inside of us to guide us in our daily actions and recognize that this will allow us to truly enjoy a rich existence in every facet (part) of our lives.

    You possess a good heart and have a great deal of love to give to those who are part of your world. It is important that you share this with others and recognize that it will be returned by them. You live in an environment that is surrounded by love. Your parents, family and friends care for you and you reflect this love. It is important to recognize that love is built upon the acts of kindness and graciousness. These two ingredients are true expressions of love: you need to always be kind in expressing your feelings to others, and gracious and generous in sharing your inner feelings and emotions.

    While I share these inner thoughts with you, I also acknowledge that sometimes your grandfather (Papa) is not always as outwardly loving as he should be in his dealing with others. It is not that I am not capable of that emotion, it is more likely that during my formative years (growing up years) I was limited by family events and my immaturity to grasp the concept of what love represents in one's life. You are in a much better position at this point in your life to truly absorb the full concept of this feeling and I am hopeful that you will embrace this feeling with enthusiasm and openness.

Love is something you should share with everyone who is an integral part of your life. It will make you a better and more complete person. Try to limit your criticisms and negative thoughts as you engage with others, knowing that acts of kindness and graciousness will enrich your life and fill it with love. Love is reciprocal. It is give and receive.

Love,
Papa & Nana
November 18, 2014

POTENTIAL

Dear Jaden,

Today I am going to share with you some of the reasons why some people fail in meeting their full potential. We all determine our own destiny (future) through our efforts to perform well. You, as a growing, evolving young person, must make a number of choices that will affect your life. I recognize that trying hard doesn't always guarantee success. Success is often a fluky (mixed bag) depending as much on luck and favor as on hard work. But, while hard work may not guarantee success, not working hard always guarantees failure.

As a young man growing up, I faced many difficult struggles and I recognized early that any road that I wished to follow to become a successful adult would not be easy and not without cost. While we all need breaks and good fortune to achieve, we must also recognize that working hard is its own reward. It affirms (identifies) you as a person and lights the way for others to see you for the person you are and can be.

For all people life is a hill. You can either climb or stay at the bottom. This may not be fair or even right but the reality of it is that some people are born at the bottom of the hill and others at the middle or top of it. You are very fortunate because you have been provided with many positives that will support you well in your development as a person. The major obstacle you face is how to take advantage of these positives (i.e. schooling, personality, physical appearance and a variety of innate skills) to make certain that you grow into adulthood with the ability and drive to help make your life and others' productive and meaningful.

Working hard should not be an option for you. It is something you need to achieve and incorporate into your being. It starts early in life and becomes more and more important as you move through your educational experiences at school. As I said before, it will identify you as a person who can accept challenges. Today, as you work in your classroom at school, you are provided with a rich opportunity to develop that "hard working" capacity. For example, when given a mathematical problem or asked to write an essay (composition) about a topic you need to give this assignment all the necessary time and effort to make certain that it represents your best work. Rushing through an activity doesn't allow anyone to do his best. Hard work means giving your "all" to any challenge presented. You may not have the right answer all the time, but it won't be for a lack of effort.

In closing, I am urging you to always try hard and not take things for granted because they appear easy. You might be distracted by other things (TV, computers, sports, etc.) but it is important to remember that there is a time and place for everything in your life and your ability to make the right choices will make the difference. Like all successful people you need to work hard. Your trip up the ladder will be made much easier as a result. Choose the right path.

Love
Papa & Nana
March 14, 2014

Dear Jaden,

Since we live approximately 3,000 miles apart (NYC to LA) this distance has afforded us limited time together to allow for the opportunity to truly share and gain more intimate knowledge about each other. Distance and time, being what they are, has made me realize that it might be appropriate at this time in our letter writing experiences to allow you to get to know more about me and my "inner workings" and for you to reciprocate by sharing some of your inner thoughts with me as well. This change in direction should help to make our written "conversations" even more meaningful for each other. You can reveal as much as you like about yourself and I will do the same. Together we can discuss our strengths, our weaknesses, our feelings and, above all, how we view ourselves as functioning human beings. You can enlighten me about how you envision yourself as a growing young person, highlighting some of the private feelings you possess about yourself. You will need to explore the drives and forces that make you who you are and what you hope to become, and I will do the same from the perspective of someone who has lived much longer and experienced a bit more than you have. Mine will be a longer narrative (story) and yours will be shorter but just as meaningful. Let us begin.

As a young boy, and even now as an aging adult, I have always leaned toward being introspective, asking questions of myself about who I am and trying to appreciate and understand what makes me "tick" and be different from others. Since no two people are exactly alike (including identical twins) I sought to find my inner self, including my strengths and weaknesses. Talking to myself (not aloud but inwardly) is something I have done all my life. I enjoy those "self-conversations" since they don't include disputes, only clarifications of what I usually agree with and intend to follow. While most people see me as a "people person" because I possess the skill to speak before large groups of people, displaying a good sense of humor and a connection to the audience. But the truth of the matter is that I truly enjoy the opportunities for self-reflection which can only happen when I am spending time alone (thinking, swimming, reading, writing, and daydreaming) My career in education kept me surrounded by people (adults and children) almost all the time and as a result the few moments I was able to be alone were cherished by me. I need you to know that I do like people (all kinds) but the times spent privately were usually rewarding. A close friend of mine once described me as a submerged submarine. He said, "Every once in a while Stan would lift the periscope above the water level, look around and decide nothing of importance was going on, and lower the periscope and go off on his own." I honestly think that I am a bit more involved than that but it is not a bad portrayal of my behavior at times.

I have enjoyed the friendships of many people over the years but just a few of these would be considered strong relationships. Many of my closest colleagues (friends) were women. The educational profession provided women with many job opportunities. This was particularly true when I first entered the school system. In those days women had mainly three choices: be a secretary, a school teacher or a homemaker. As a result, I was fortunate to work with a number of female educators who shared many of my ideas and thoughts about our chosen field. Schools, particularly lower or elementary schools, need to be nurturing environments and women on the whole, appear better able to provide that needed school ingredient and that quality was one that I connected with. I also think that the loss of my mother played a role in my choice of friends. There is a female gene (trait) that is embedded in all people, including men (my opinion). Some reject it as an affront to their masculinity while others accept it. I was in the latter category and felt strongly that it was a factor that made me a better man, simply because empathy and sensitivity to others became an integral part of my life. It became a legacy that I believed I could pass on to my family and to the thousands of children, teachers and parents I interacted with during my life.

As a young boy I grew up in a family of meager means.

My father was a quiet, unique person. He was very reserved while my mother was the active, more responsive, outspoken member of our household (does that sound familiar?). My dad was a star athlete in high school. He was a track and field champion, a first baseman on the high school team and an accomplished swimmer who served as a life guard at a local "Y" during the summer. All of this I discovered after he died when I found a box full of medals and citations he received for his athletic accomplishments. He never shared that with us and I regret that oversight. My mother, Lillian, was a Russian immigrant and 16 years old when she married my father (he was 20). I was born after their first year of marriage, my brother Gil followed a year later and your uncle Les (Adam's father) was the baby brother born 13 years later. We lived in the Bronx and moved to Coney Island in Brooklyn when I was of school age. We were not doing well financially because my dad was not well at that time and suffered from a number of ailments that limited his employment opportunities. When I reached high school age, I got a job as an usher at a local movie house and worked evenings and weekends to help meet some of the financial needs of our family. When I reached college age (eighteen) my father was given a job in a sporting goods store owned by his younger brother (my uncle). Life got a bit better and I was able to go to college as long as I took care of all my school expenses (tuition, etc.). I worked as a waiter/bus boy in a hotel in the Catskill Mountains (often called the Jewish Alps) during each year I was a student at NYU studying to become a teacher, and made enough money to meet the costs of going to college including living expenses.

Unfortunately our parents passed away as I was entering my senior year at college. My mother died first and my dad joined her ten months later. It was a very difficult period of time in our lives. Leslie was 1 year old, Gil was 20 and I was 21. I won't burden you with all the details of this devastating happening, except to share with you my initial feelings about God and my exposure to a ritual that I had to follow for almost two years that impacted my life forever.

69

In the Jewish religion it is expected that the oldest son in the family attend religious services every day for a year to repeat the mourner's prayer (Kaddish) after the death of a parent. The Rabbi shared that with me and suggested that I be at the synagogue in the morning and evening each day to recite the prayer in their honor. I did this for almost two years in spite of the anger and deep resentment I felt toward God for what he allowed to happen to my family. I would sit through the services each day with tears and the unfortunate events that surrounded me. I would often leave for school or home being sad or depressed. It was there that I truly learned to cry and it has been part of me ever since. Supposedly, real men don't cry but I cry often when I am touched by something that stirs my memories. Crying is an accepted feeling of emotion for all people, and I am certain that you have the security and depth of emotion to allow your feelings at a moment of sadness or sensitivity be displayed and shared.

I have always attempted to work diligently at whatever task I faced. What I may have lacked in intellect I compensated by providing more energy and desire than most people in reaching my goals. Nothing came easy and while I envy all the advantages you have (good schools, financial security, great home environment and a mountain of love surrounding you from family and friends) I would like to encourage you to accept who you are and will become with humility and respect for all people. Your grandfather (Papa) was and is a "bleeding liberal" who feels pain for those who are not as fortunate in life. I am hopeful that you will devote a good portion of your life to helping others in need and recognize your innate responsibilities toward others–all others.

The good that people do does live long after they are gone. Keep that in mind as you enjoy your life by living fully every day with direction and good feeling for those who pass through your life.

I look forward to reading your story at this early stage in your life. You will be 12 years old shortly and it would be interesting to learn about your feelings during your voyage to maturity. Enjoy the trip!

Love
Papa & Nana
December 21, 2015

WHEN A FRIEND MOVES

Dear Jaden,

Today we are going to communicate about the issue of "losing a friend" due to the fact that he or she will be moving to a new and distant place. I truly appreciate how you must have felt about your friend moving to Texas. It was a genuine feeling of loss for you when he and his family decided to relocate, and I am pleased to have learned that you felt so deeply about the situation that you were fighting tears as you said goodbye to him.

Crying or having your eyes "water up" because you feel so deeply about something is really a positive trait that sensitive people feel and possess and it reflects a deep and caring understanding for others. It is really alright to feel deeply enough to express emotion in a positive way. You come from a family of criers. Your grandfather (Papa) has done his share of crying and I am certain that your stoic father has left the need to cry at some juncture in his life. Crying is not a "female thing", although your mother, grandmother Nana and your Aunt Lilly are quite exceptional in this area. In fact, the Seidman Family has gained a well-known reputation in this area.

In your lifetime, many people will come and go through your journey on earth. Those who really care about you, and who you carry the same feelings for, will remain as life-long friends. There is a good chance that you and your friend will connect again in the future and this prospect can be enhanced if you maintain a form of communication with him over the years you are apart, for example, written letters or emails, telephone calls, computer contacts, visits to his family and a score of other forms of communication will allow you to remain in touch with him. If it is a friendship you want to maintain, there are lots of avenues you can follow to keep his friendship.

Friends are important for all people. They often define the person you are and provide the impetus and foundation for you to grow and prosper.

Your growth to maturity will include many different kinds of people who will appeal or not appeal to you. The ones you care for, you will cherish and make certain that those relationships will be lasting ones. This might be the case with you and your friend. It is a decision you both have to make.

You possess a very sincere, endeavoring personality and the opportunities you will have to cultivate friends will be huge. Friends are important for all people. They often define the person you are and provide the impetus and foundation for you to grow and prosper. In many ways, they become family and enrich your life. It is not always easy to build a lasting and mutually beneficial friendship. You will learn that skill in time. While waiting for that to happen you should do everything possible to enjoy your friends. You accomplish that by respecting them as people with all the differences they present, such as race, color, religion, personality, interests, etc. This will allow you to embrace people for who they are and how they contribute to the welfare and growth of you as a person.

Friendship can be forever. So choose wisely and well. Keep in mind that friendship is a two way street. You need to learn how to "give and take" in positive ways in all your relationships. I strongly encourage you to develop deep and feeling friendships even if it means that you have to cry a bit.

Love,
Papa & Nana
March 29, 2014

o cool that your mother wo
sional in her chosen field
not that many years ago
boy of your age) that havin
as professionals was frowne
employment opportunities a
weve as a secretary in an c
in a hospital, a teacher in
mother at home raising chi
limited and unfair environ
seeking to be independent
owners. This unfortunate situ
ble for a huge waste of hum
tge and made women like yo
cond class citizens. Their exis
e good will and generosity o
their husbands. This was t
nd mother (Nana) and others
ve young women and as a
d to live as second class ci

CHAPTER 3

On Humanity

Letters on Treating Others with Respect and Kindness

Dear Jaden,

I was pleased to hear that you enjoyed your vacation to Tahiti with your mom and dad. You are really a fortunate young man and I am certain that you appreciate all of the different advantages that have been provided for you in your young life thus far. It is rewarding to know that you have grown and developed so beautifully in such an enriched environment.

We all possess distinctive personalities and since no one is perfect, it is important to evaluate who we are as people and measure our strengths and weaknesses reflected in our daily activities with the people who are part of our lives (for example, parents, friends, relatives, etc.).

Your parents recently mentioned to me how pleased they are with your development as a growing person and while they were very complimentary about you, they did feel that there was one area that you need to address to further enhance your sophisticated social skills with your relationships with others.

They felt that on occasion, you felt the need to assume a "bossy" attitude when communicating about an issue or feeling where one has to assert himself, in order to make certain that his opinions or feelings are known and appreciated by others (particularly during a difference of opinion about an issue). We all have to learn to be sensitive to the feelings of others and to recognize that there will be times when others might not be in agreement with you and that this difference should be met with understanding and sensitivity and respect. We can't always have "our way" and it is vital that we learn to appreciate how to deal other peoples' feelings, opinions and actions.

Sometimes when people get "bossy", it is because they feel insecure or uncertain about the problem or issue they are facing. You are very bright and articulate, but you have to learn that an open, frank discussion in which there is "give and take" might be a more appropriate approach to reaching an understanding in your dealings with you parents and others.

It is important to assert yourself, especially when you feel passionately about your point of view, but it shouldn't be done without showing respect for the rights of the other person or persons. A good "boss" is somebody people like because he is open and accepting of other people's feelings and he respects their rights to feel and think differently. You possess all those positive qualities and now it has become appropriate for you to use your personal skills with a sensitivity that leads to real communication with others. It is part of you and you are moving in that direction. Use your mother as your role model.

Love,
Papa & Nana
July 24, 2014

BULLY

Dear Jaden,

My letter to you today is about a subject that has recently attracted a great deal of attention. It is about the "bully" and how to deal with people who hurt the feelings of others and often abuse people physically and emotionally. There will be number of "bullies" that you will meet in your life and it is important that you recognize who they are and learn how to deal with them appropriately.

The dictionary definition of a bully is: "A person who is mean or cruel to weaker people." It is usually someone who disrespects others and tries to intimidate people to "bow to his will." He or she is usually not a nice or likable person and uses his "might" to make people feel weak or inadequate. In many ways the bully is often a coward who uses this angry, ugly approach to hide his (or her) own feelings of being dissatisfied or unhappy with who he or she is as a person. These are individuals you should try to avoid and ignore. Unfortunately they do exist and you will be exposed to them at school, in your neighborhood, at work when you are older and during all kinds of social activities where people gather and meet. You don't have to look for them but you should be alert to how to deal with them when you have the misfortune to meet them.

If at all possible, you should attempt to disassociate yourself from their presence and seek the friendship of those you respect and like whenever possible. In the rare moment that you have to communicate with a bully, it would be wise to keep your "cool", speak softly and directly and let him then know that you deserve to be respected as a fellow human being and that your feelings and point of view should be acknowledged to the same extent that you are accepting of his (her) opinions and thoughts. Mutual respect and understanding should be expected from both parties. Keep in mind that the bully is not a "strong" person, but one who uses this technique to merely intimidate and it is important for you to remain resolute (firm) in your convictions so that your position in any conflict or disagreement is heard and appreciated. Most bullies won't fight. Screaming negative and abusive words are what they do best. You need to stay above that and be satisfied that you have made your position known in a convincing manner and that you hold no ill feelings toward the bully. However, you should expect that respect and understanding are mutual.

One last item that I would like to pass on to you is the importance for you to recognize. Whenever you see a friend or some person being bullied, it is proper for you to move to the defense of this person. You are not seeking a fight, but you are demanding that all people (friends and others) be treated in a civil and appropriate fashion. I show love for others when we provide support and care for them. There are all kinds of people in the world and you will select many friends that you hold close to your heart and, in addition, you will need to always be able to show respect and display a positive feel for all people who come in and out of your life. Good Luck!!

Love,
Papa & Nana
January 17, 2014

DON'T JUDGE A BOOK BY ITS COVER

Dear Jaden,

There was a book I recently read and I would like to share a line from the story with you and discuss the reason I felt made it such a meaningful and appropriate thought for all of us to share. It reads as follows: "Beauty is an enormous unmerited (not deserved) gift given randomly, stupidly." What is being said by this writer is that if someone is born beautiful or handsome it is merely their good fortune and not something that they had accomplished through their efforts. Actually it is basically a mixture of genes that people inherit from their family "tree" and while it can be a decided advantage in life, it should not define a person. There are and have been many, many people who have lived productive and achieving lives without having the advantages of being physically attractive and, might I add, that there have been others who have suffered disabilities through disease, accidents and birth defects who are part of that group. I guess I am saying that you shouldn't judge a book by its cover, and now that you have become a reader that can appreciate that it is the "inside pages" (core of the book) that matters as it should be with the personality, intelligence and social sense of the people you choose to surround yourself with.

Those are much more important than the "glitz" (shine) of any outside physical matter being presented.

You are handsome young man and that is a gift, but you have to grow to recognize that it will require much more than that to be recognized as a contributing, positive force in the world you choose to become a part of. The qualities of sensitivity to the needs of others, compassion for others and respect for the differences that people reflect in their race, color, religion, opinion, lifestyles and the thousands of other ways that separate people to make then unique. You shouldn't be judgmental of others but accepting of the fact that each of them is an individual who possesses qualities, interests, needs and feelings that make them who they are, and that must be appreciated and loved.

I urge you to be especially open to those less fortunate than you. You are growing up as part of a family that strongly believes that all people are special and deserve to be treated with warmth and understanding. It is obvious that there will be some people who won't appeal to you as potential friends or colleagues, however it is important for you to remember to be as positive as you can in whatever capacity they appear in your life.

You will be long remembered for all the efforts you have made to help make life more accepting and rewarding for others than how "handsome" you appear to people. Good looks are transitory (don't last forever) but good deeds and love go on and on and on!

Love,
Papa & Nana
August 2, 2014

Dear Jaden,

Today I am going to try to write you a letter about the meaning of friendship and the role it will play in your life. Making healthy choices of people you wish to befriend, and being a friend to those same people, requires a lot of effort, good feelings and understanding on your part. Being a good friend and enjoying the pleasure of having good friends who care for you will truly make you a happier and better person. Allow me to present some ideas and thoughts I have about this subject that might be of some value to you.

A. To be a good friend to someone means you have to accept them with all the positive and negative characteristics (features) he or she might possess. Since no one is perfect (except for you) you need to realize that you must accept people for who they are and not what you would like them to be. You don't judge them but appreciate their individual differences, points of view and lifestyles.

B. You need to be warm and giving with your friends and learn about their interests and goals so that you can support them in their efforts to grow as people. Be open to them and sincere in supporting their hopes and aspirations.

C. You must use your words in conversations with friends to support their needs. Be open and honest with them and not judgmental. People are attracted to those who share similar interests and beliefs. However, you can still be good friends with people who are different as long as you are appreciative of the differences and respectful of their rights to enjoy their own opinions and views.

D. People like to be friendly with individuals who feel good about themselves and have a positive "glow" (feeling) about who they are. When you feel secure and happy you become more attractive to others and as a result, want to have you as a friend. Unhappy and grumpy people have very few friends. We all like to be around people who possess a positive outlook on life. 81

In closing, healthful relationships with friends are an important part of every person's life. You are fortunate because you have all the ingredients to be a good friend to many people. You are smart, nice looking, humorous (funny), caring and loaded with personality. These are gifts that should not be wasted. You need to reach out to all kinds of people, particularly those who are less fortunate and try to make their lives better and more fulfilling. You gain more by giving than by receiving. This is something that you will learn as you develop and grow as a person. Friends should be cherished for life and you will be happy and enhanced as a result of your ability to make and keep friendships.

I wish you well.
Love,
Papa & Nana
December 12, 2013

JUST SAY NO

Dear Jaden,

I am going to share my thoughts about a very difficult and somewhat removed topic that will grow more in importance as you grow older and play a vital and more meaningful role in your life. Learning to say "No" appropriately has become a very vital language skill to master in our present environment. We all possess the need to please the people who surround us and almost all the time that is a very admirable and correct thing to do. Most of us choose to join groups and to cultivate (grow) friendships with people we like or love. This is particularly evident as we move through our early stages of development when we are in the process of discovering who we are as a person and what our self-concept has evolved into. In other words, what we feel about ourselves as a functioning individual.

You are approaching that stage now, and in the near future you will have to master the skill of knowing when to say No appropriately to situations and people who might be harmful to your very being. This issue appears at the pre-teen and teen-age years for most people and you are approaching that level rapidly.

Because you have good relationships with your parents and because most, if not all of your needs (physical, social and emotional) are being addressed and hopefully being met with positive results, your transition (movement) to making positive and healthful decisions about your wellbeing should be easily attained (reached). Your parents have laid a foundation for you which will help you in this direction.

You will be making decisions that will affect your future life as you move through your developing years into emerging adulthood. Decisions about your future world of work, your relationships with members of the opposite sex, and the impending lure of tobacco, drugs and other forms of addiction will have been made easier for you due to your upbringing, your ego development, your relationships you enjoy with your family and circle of friends, and your ability to determine what is right and what is wrong.

Saying No to drugs, smoking, drinking, bullying, abusive behavior and other negative actions is something you should be able to achieve and appreciate. You possess all the ingredients that maintain a wholesome, productive life full of happiness as you grow to maturity. Learn from observing others (family, friends, etc.) and use it as a tool to enable you to enjoy a substantial and happy life.

I urge you to start thinking about how to say No appropriately to circumstances that are harmful to you. You make the decisions that will guide your life. Make them well with understanding and a warm, good feeling about yourself.

Love,
Papa & Nana
September 18, 2014

Dear Jaden,

The concept of leadership and the role it plays in all of our lives is a subject I would like to share with you at this time. Since I feel that you have the potential to become a leader, or at least perform in a leadership capacity at some time in your life, I thought that it might be of some value for you to consider the responsibilities that surround this opportunity.

Some people feel that leaders are born with the needed skills to assume that role and while I agree that there are people who seem to possess the innate ingredients to develop leadership qualities, I also believe that most leaders develop because they have an ability to relate on a positive basis to people and who are placed in situations that are often created to encourage those with that particular inclination (learning) to emerge. A leader does not have to be forceful and all knowing. He or she must however, be able to be sensitive to the needs of others and provide a sense of security that permeates (fills) the environment of the group he (she) is guiding to reach their common goals.

There are good leaders and bad ones. The negative leader uses a forceful personality and often fear and anger to promote people to do awful things. Think about the dictator Adolf Hitler and the role he played in manipulating his huge army of men to destroy the lives of 6 million Jews, or the present leaders of Isis in the Middle East who use the brutal beheadings and killings of their prisoners in captivity to gain negative control over people. There are damaged and vile leaders who use the force of evil to accomplish their ugly goals. Leadership is truly a responsibility to guide and help others to a better understanding and fulfillment in reaching goals that make life more meaningful and richer. It should never be used to abuse or vilify others.

Enough of that. Now let's concentrate on the positive values of leadership and how you can use these values when you are placed in a role of leadership (for example, as the president of your

84

class, as a captain of a sports team, as a chairperson of a school committee, etc.) First of all, you need to be secure with who you are as a person. If you like yourself and receive positive vibes from others then you can look forward to achieving success as a leader. You need to know how to respond to those who disagree with you. Upset and anger never work. Always respect what is broached (suggested) by others and learn to be a good listener. Take other people's words and thoughts and share them with others. You don't know everything and often others will have good ideas and thoughts that should be incorporated (included) in whatever plan of action you and your group decide is the approach or answer to an issue of concern. You have a strong and convincing voice but you must recognize that you are not always right in all situations. Compromise and acceptance of the feelings of others can perform miracles in accomplishing what you feel is appropriate action.

It is easier to be a "follower". You make no decisions and often have the opportunity to blame others (i.e. the leader) for mistakes that might occur. As a leader, you will need to learn that you can't win all the battles. In fact, sometimes a loss can help to lay a foundation for a future victory. All you do is to help create an environment for understanding and appreciation of all opinions and courses of action. A good leader leads from the front and accepts graciously all the praise and blame for whatever takes place. No one will win every debate, argument or battle. A true leader knows how to lose with grace and win with empathy (good feeling to others).

Leadership opportunities will come to those who appreciate differences and who welcome debate and other points of view. I have no doubt that you will be be given leadership opportunities. Enjoy that responsibility by knowing who are and how meaningful and important are the people who surround you.

Best of luck,
Papa & Nana
March 6, 2015

Dear Jaden,

I hope you are well and looking forward to your winter break from school. Nana and I are looking forward to seeing you soon for the holidays.

Today's letter will be devoted to "why it is so cool that your mother works as a professional in her chosen field of endeavor." It was not that many years ago (when I was a bot of your age) that having women work as professionals was frowned upon. The only employment opportunities available to them were as a secretary in an office, a nurse in a hospital, a teacher in school or as a mother at home raiding children. It was a limited and unfair environment for women seeking to be independent and productive was earners. This unfortunate situation was responsible for a huge waste of human skill and knowledge and made women like your mother into second class citizens. Their existence depended upon the good will and generosity of their families and, or their husbands. This was the dilemma you grandmother (Nana) and others faced when they were young woman and as a result were subjected to live as second class citizens with little opportunity to grow and develop into contributing members of our society.

Fortunately, in the 1960's women banded together and fought for women's rights which helped to change our world. Today woman are playing major roles in all segments of life (for example, as doctors, lawyers, politicians and in every profession). Your mother has been part of this revolution and you should be proud of what she has accomplished. She has been very successful in the different fields of endeavor she chose and as a result she has, with the support of your father been able to help provide you with a life style that is productive and rich in opportunity. All people are born with the need to climb a mountain to be successful in life. Some are born on the bottom of the ladder (hill) fighting all their lives to get out of poverty, some are born in the middle of the hill having some advantages in their middle class lives and others are born at the top of the hill and are "doomed" to succeed. Your mother works hard to make certain that you have all the needed tools to be successful in life. You are one "lucky boy" while I recognize that you would like to have more of her time at home, it is important to keep in mind that it is not the number of hours on spends with someone that matters, but how meaningful and positive the time is spent when you are together. Your mom's work has enriched her life and, in time, your life as well.

It is "cool" that your mother is a successful professional in work and in motherhood. You benefit immensely from her efforts and should cherish the time you have together. In the near future you will be able to fully understand the importance of being a well rounded and complete person. This is your mother's ambition for you and you are fortunate to be "along for the ride".

Love,
Papa & Nana
December 3, 2013

POLITICS

Dear Jaden,

Today I would like to share with you my feelings about "politics" and how this process effects our lives. It is a bit different from our previous letters, but one I hope you will enjoy. Every four years our country faces the dilemma of electing a president who will provide the needed leadership to guide our nation for the next four years. It is usually a "battle" between the two main parties labeled as Democrats and Republicans, although on occasion, there can be an Independent candidate who might be added to this list as an additional possibility. This occurs rarely. It is usually the two main political organizations (Democratic & Republican) who control this process and one part will eventually emerge as the "winner" and as a result have his or her candidate as the elected President of the United States. This has been the history of our country in its selection of its leaders since the birth of our nation. This procedure, in my mind, leaves a great deal to be desired and I will try to elaborate and present my point of view regarding this important process.

I recognize that our democratic voting procedure is the best approach in selecting leadership that presently exists in our present day world, particularly when comparing it to other countries' forms of government like Communism, kingdoms, dictatorships, etc. I merely feel that our potential proces, as we are now observing in the recent presidential campaign, leaves much to be desired and to improve. This needs to be addressed before it leads us astray from the original goals provided by our forefathers who wrote our Constitution, our Bill of Rights and all the guidelines that helped to create our great country.

We need to reassert and teach our population (starting in elementary school) about the need for civility (code of behavior) in addressing the issues our country is facing. We need to stop disparaging (insulting) people because of color, race ethnicities, sexual orientation, religious beliefs and denying the need to provide for women's rights, supporting the poor. Poverty must be eradicated (removed) from our country. There is much more that can be included but attention to the above mentioned items would be a great step forward.

I present my feeling regarding the world of politics to you with the intention of helping you appreciate the problems our present political operation presents. You can become a Republican, a Democrat or an Independent but whatever category you choose, you must treat that responsibility with maturity and respect and not follow the dictates of those who have little or no regard for the political process as it should exist in our country. Respect the rights of those who oppose your political position and use your strength and positive fervor to foster a position without rancor (bitterness) and ill feeling.

88

I urge you to help make our political world of the future a more receptive and supportive platform for all members of the society you inhabit. We, as a country, and you, as an individual, will not be able to move forward until we meet as a total entirety (complete group) to move forward to meet our responsibilities as caring and responsive human beings.

Love,
Papa & Nana
February 3, 2016

PREJUDICE

Dear Jaden,

Congratulations on your excellent report card you received from school. You should be very proud of your accomplishments and we look forward to your continued success at school and in life.

Today I would like to share some thoughts about how bias (prejudice) can affect the world in which you live and how you can best respond to the harmful impact this "disease" might have upon your life as you grow and develop into a man.

Prejudice is a form of hate that is heavily embedded (rooted) in people who are insecure, self-centered, weak-minded and often lacking a healthful self-concept about who they are as functioning persons. Bias is often observed when individuals or groups see people who are different from them as threats to their wellbeing. They often dislike them for unfounded reasons involving an unhealthy rationale which rejects people for being different in their appearance, for living different lifestyles, for having different backgrounds and religious beliefs, and for possessing differences in skin color, sexual orientation and a host of other traits that are viewed as negative in their limited view of life.

It is important that you learn to respect and enjoy the "world of differences" which will enhance you and be part of your entire life. The beauty and joy of having a productive and meaningful existence on earth is being able to incorporate (digest) all the segments of the environment you are part of and experience the beauty of others and the full scope of the world. You are living in a country (USA) that has been slow in erasing the concept of prejudice. We have made some progress in areas such as racial relationships, sexual orientation, women's rights, etc. but we still have a long way to go before all of us have the ability to appreciate the many differences that make all of us unique and very special. I have faith in you and your peers to bridge the gap that still exists in our society regarding the acceptance and love of all people regardless of whatever differences they might reflect. Actually, everyone of us is unique (different) and that should be appreciated. No two people are exactly alike and the difference that we see in each other's physical traits, personalities, interests, backgrounds, and all the other factors that form the lives of all people should be accepted and appreciated by all.

It is vital that you don't judge someone based upon what you have heard from others or from an opinion or feeling you meet. Even the most difficult man or woman possesses something appealing to respond to and it is your responsibility to find it. You need to build upon those positives and form relationships that are filled with promise and not distrust. Protect your friends from those who are bigoted and are often cruel to those who appear different and weak. Your concern and love for others will make you a more complete person in all your relationships.

Learn to extend yourself to others to support them during good and bad times and recognize that in doing this you are offering a part of yourself to the many who will come in and out of your life. This will remain with them forever. We touch people in many ways and this is the most memorable approach.

90

Please accept others for who they are and enjoy and love them for what they bring to your life. You are a most fortunate young boy who will grow to impact many lives. It is important that you don't allow prejudice and negativity to become part of your life. My hope and wish for you is that the world you will be inheriting will grow to become a more responsive and healthful environment for all people and that you will play a small role in making this possible.

Love
Papa & Nana
March 8, 2014

RELATIONSHIPS

Dear Jaden
Today I will try to explain to you the meaning and importance of the relationships you will enjoy with all sorts of people as you grow into adulthood. Wholesome relationships with others will vary (change) as you mature and they will play a major role in forming your personality as a social being.

When you are very young (birth to 8 years of age) your total world revolves around your family (parents, siblings, grandparents, aunts, uncles, cousins, etc.) and as a rule their relationships are very nurturing, warm and supportive. These family relations remain quite important to you as you age but lessen in its intensity as you grow older and enter your pre-teen and teen years. In other words, your social world increases and the friends (boys and girls) from school and other areas of your interests (sports, academics, etc.) play a larger role in your life. Being part of a group for example, classmates at school, members of a team or any other community that encourages you to participate in a group activity, becomes a paramount (most important) part of your pre-adolescent to adolescent life. Interest in girls starts to become a factor and your school life and social life becomes a bit more complex and challenging. Since girls mature earlier than boys, their interests and predilictions (preferences) differ from yours at this particular stage in your life. Allow me to give you an example of what I mean. When I was a boy in the sixth grade my main interests revolved around school work, playing football, baseball and basketball or just hanging around with my friends. One day while I was walking around the classroom, a girl quietly pushed me into the clothing closet and kissed me. I got embarrassed and ran out of the classroom not knowing how and why this happened. What I didn't realize at that time was that girls mature earlier than boys and my readiness was not there. I share this with you because I am certain that you are beginning to see the differences in the maturity levels between the boys and girls in your present class at this time. Girls grow up faster than we (males) do, but we do catch up with them in time (at least some of us do).

The relationship you develop as a boy with all kinds of people will help to define you as a person. It is important that you learn to "give and take" in your activities with the people you surround yourself with, as you grow older you will be attracted to many different kinds of people and this will include men and women. Many of my best friends were women and they played a major role in my life. You learn to enjoy all of them for what they bring to your life (i.e. good feelings, friendship, values, energy and love). You grow to appreciate their strengths, weaknesses and characteristics that make them unique and important to you. You will have to learn to allow people to get to know you as a person (the good and the bad) to enable you to grow as a sensitive, giving individual.

Enjoying good, positive feelings with all kinds of people can be difficult but the reward of being able to share feelings, interests, thoughts and love with others will make you a "rich" man. Good luck in your efforts to reach that goal.

92

P.S. The girl who kissed me in the closet when I was in sixth grade was Arlene Rose. I never saw her after we graduated public school. I met your grandmother (Nana) much later.

Love,
Papa & Nana
September 15, 2014

SPORTSMANSHIP

Dear Jaden,

This week's topic will be "sportsmanship" or knowing how to win or lose with grace and good feeling. In today's world the athletes, our leaders and the people we most admire (athletes, politicians, family members and even friends) have created an improper and unwholesome image of what good sportsmanship should mean and exemplify.

We have grown to accept people pounding their chests or sticking their faces into the faces of their opponents with a strong sentiment that states, "See that–I'm better than you." The concept of showing respect for the opposing member of a team that you are playing has disappeared and the new approach of "in your face" and demeaning your opponents has become the symbol of winning or achieving your goal whether it be in sports or in our daily lives.

In my eyes, this cultural change has made all of us a lot less as human beings and has unfortunately moved us a lot closer to the behavior patterns of other forms of life (animal life, etc.) where respect for the dignity of others and self is missing in their forms of communication. Hopefully, we should have developed beyond that stage.

93

Winning a game or achieving an advantage over an adversary (opponent) isn't the only means of establishing yourself as a person of importance or significance. We all would rather win than lose in whatever situation we find ourselves involved. However, winning isn't everything and often after a loss to a worthy individual or team you can learn a great deal about yourself and the "game of life" that you are living each day. Going through antics like (in your face or thumping your chest) doesn't make you stronger or a better person because you need to learn that there are many ups and downs in all sports, and in life as well, and the person who learns from his (or her) defeats and who gains respect from others for the manner in which he conducts himself, whether winning or losing, will inevitably be a more successful and complete human being.

Showing good sportsmanship toward another person by not belittling an opponent's efforts makes your winning achievement more meaningful and enhances you as a person. Always show respect to your opponent (sports or in other areas of endeavor). It makes you more complete as a functioning being and better prepares you for a life full of meaningful success.

As for the losses you must endure in life, they can be used to help you appreciate how fortunate you were to have had the caring and loving experiences with all kinds of people who came and went in your days on earth. They all will remember and cherish you as a complete person who not only won at most activities in life, but also knew how to lose graciously.

In closing, allow me to encourage you to love the times you've won and appreciate and learn from your defeats, but always show humility and appreciation to all.

Love,
Papa and Nana
December 23, 2013

TEAMWORK

Dear Papa,

 Teamwork is the thing that gets people to work together and helps people expand their horizons while working with others. When people work together, they become open to new ideas. New ideas help create the best things in the world. Making these ideas can sometimes be hard, but it helps to have someone else to bounce ideas with. Working as a team with someone else may sometimes be difficult; you always have to find ways to listen to each other's ideas. In athletics, no point guard, quarterback, or team leaders build the team chemistry right away. These leaders have to bring everybody together to be able to work as a team. When teams start to play well, it most likely means that their team chemistry level is high. They can really rely on each other and relax because they know that their team has their back. This does not just apply in sports. It can apply in everyday life too: on a school project, at work, and at home with your family.

The best teamwork in the world is found in strong families. This is true because they know each other's strengths and weaknesses. Since they know these things, they can help support each other's strengths and help each other grow on their weaknesses. When at work, the same mind set applies. You have to rely on others to sort of be your family out of your family. You have to make sure that you can benefit others around you by being a supportive friend, family member, and person in general. When at school, it may be harder because sometimes kids don't fully want to help everyone around them. But, the more selfless you are, the better you and others around you feel.

If you want to have a good team, you need to learn to not just be an individual, but to work as a unit. Working as a unit requires practice and communication. If two people who don't work great together get assigned a project, they can still do well with hard work. If they work great on two individual parts of a project, they may succeed, but there would be less teamwork involved.

Teams have retreats to get to know each other better and see each other from different angles. On retreats, it also helps get teams' minds off of what they are doing; that lets them enjoy the experience and have fun. After retreats, teams become better friends, which gives them better communication. Better communication gives teams better collaboration, and that gives teams better teamwork.

Creating a spirit of teamwork on projects is hard. I am more of a "if you want something done right, do it yourself" kind of person. When someone does not do their part, it is hard to confront them. It is also hard to manage time. Having different ideas can sometimes be a killer to a team project. When there is a time crunch and people won't change their original ideas, it can make deciding on an idea that both people like very difficult. Even if both writers or workers are great, if the ideas are different, it is hard to collaborate or combine the ideas. Like if you have a story about a break dancing elephant and a sun that blows up and makes new solar systems. Both are great ideas, but very different. It would be extremely difficult to combine these ideas.

JFK wanted people who disagreed with him in his cabinet. I think that this is smart and not smart. It is not smart because the president already has enough stress in his life. It is smart because when there are disagreements, conversations become deeper and more interesting. Better ideas come from deeper conversations. Also, the teamwork has to be stronger in order to have an idea that everybody to the smallest level agrees on. If I were president, I would have more people in my cabinet who do not agree with me. I would do this so the people who don't agree with me and the people who do agree with me have their ideas collide and make better ones. Since there would be close to an even split in my cabinet, there would be an equal say in the topic at hand.

So Papa, have you ever had a team project where you had to do a lot more work than the other person? Did it annoy you? If you were president, what would your cabinet be like? Would you have people who agree with you or people who disagreed with you?

Love,
Jaden

∾⤬∿

Dear Jaden,

I truly enjoyed reading your recent letter about the "meaning of teamwork". Your concept about people working together to achieve new and better ideas to create things that will improve the world is right on target. You also wisely recognized that working with others while attempting to solve problems can be difficult at times, but that often when good minds operate in harmony much more can be accomplished than can be done by an individual who works independently. The importance of being receptive to other people's ideas and the willingness to work as a member of a team has many rewards. As you suggested in your letter, it takes "team chemistry" among players on an athletic team to produce positive results and this was a fine illustration of obtaining a maximum result due to the combined efforts of all. Teamwork is needed in sports and in all walks of our life.

I loved the way you described the importance of teamwork among families. The need to be supportive of family members, friends or schoolmates when addressing the making of a group decision does provide the foundation for a wise decision about any issue you may be facing. By you being selfless (a good word) in this process it does help make you and others feel more secure and pleased with the final outcome of whatever the event or issue might be.

The use of retreats for the purpose of developing a better system of communication was another wise suggestion on your part and it does bring people (teams, etc) together for the purpose of establishing good morale and positive vibes (feelings) working toward common goals.

I am pleased that you see yourself as a "if you want to or get something done, do it yourself' kind of guy and that is very understandable but it really thrills me that you also recognize that collaborating with others can be more rewarding and successful if your approach in this process is done in a positive and accepting manner. Congratulations, you have developed and grown to become a thinking and feeling person. However, you must continue to recognize some of the pit falls (difficulties) of working with groups (others), while wisely understanding that what can be accomplished by being a part of a cooperative working group can be more rewarding and ultimately a more successful experience for all involved.

Your reference to JFK and his penchant (learning) to include people who disagree with him as part of his cabinet does have some merits and negatives attached to it, but the fact that these people can add some thoughts and suggestions to enhance the final decisions will help make it more inclusive and meaningful to all concerned. Better ideas do come from deep discussions which include all points of view to be presented and appreciated. A "heated" discussion among all cabinet members would probably make the final decision to be reached a more meaningful and correct one. The ability to use that approach makes the President a wiser and better decision maker. If I were President, I would follow the recommendation that you suggested and include a number of dissenting people (those who might disagree with my policies) to assist me in making a decision that would be more reflective of all the people in our country. As the president of the USA, I would want to have all views to be expressed and to make certain that any decision that would be made should be reached after a thorough review of all the facts and information available. No one person is smarter than the combined efforts of a well represented and knowledgeable group.

As the head of a number of schools that I recently wrote about in my "long" letter last week there were times when I had to make difficult decisions regarding the children, parents and staff members at each of these schools. My decisions during difficult periods were always based upon what I (in consultation with others) felt would be best for all the people connected with the individual school. Some decisions are more difficult than others but it is that leader's responsibility to select a path that is n keeping with his philosophy of life which must include providing for the needs and welfare of others. It is a difficult path and process to fully appreciate until you are forced in a position that requires a decision that will affect you and others. It is challenging but if you follow the many suggestions you made in your teamwork letter then you can feel secure that you have done the right thing. I feel very strongly that you are moving very positively toward becoming a person who will be equal to any task you face.

Your writings are getting better and better and your insight and thoughts about the world around you reflect good thinking, a sensitive nature and a love for learning. Keep at it. Your report card at school is a reflection of the growth you have made over the years. Your potential for further growth and development is unlimited.

Love
Papa & Nana
December 15, 2015

...lings about the role family pla...
...portance of family and the s...
...dy of people have in molding...
... is a major factor in determ...
...e as a functioning person in...
...bviously, the most important p...
...ill be your parents. They will f...
...ant ingredients that will promote...
...ble you to develop into a caring...
...sful man. They nuture you, fee...
...ur physical, social and emotional...
...p and grow up. How well they...
...ibilities will determine what...
...ill be. I trust that you know...
...ood hands" and that they will...
...uve that your movement and...
...y to adulthood will be accom...
...love, patience, and support...
...tion and process as positive as...
...upbringing and commitment...
...sill become the foundation that...
...entire life. Once again, I ha...

CHAPTER 4

A Fulfilled Life

Letters on Living with Meaning

Dear Jaden,

Happy Birthday!! I hope you are enjoying your day with your parents and friends. Today, I thought that I would like to share with you some art work that your Nana and I did recently at an art class that we both attended. They (both paintings) are included in this letter.

Art is an area of learning that offers you an opportunity to be creative and free in expressing you inner feelings. When I went to school, the teacher of art insisted that when you were drawing or painting a picture that you were to use straight lines and present on exact duplication of what you were trying to develop. There was little time or room for creativity or being able to express yourself in your art work. It is very different today and you as a student are now given greater latitude (opportunity) to be able to project your inner feelings and personality in the art work you create. There is much more acceptance and appreciation for all kinds of art work and this includes an opportunity. For an artist or student to use a larger variety of materials and different forms of media. Art at school has become much more meaningful and reflective of the students' personalities and feelings. Judgment of what is good or bad is put aside and much more freedom is given to the student (you) to create and emote his (or her) feelings.

I am hoping that the field of art will play a role in your life. You don't have to be an accomplished artist to appreciate the vast amount of art work that is part of your environment. For example, such things as paintings, carvings, sculptures, fabrics, videos, clothing and a host of other items could be included. It should become your job to allow the world of art to enhance your life physically and emotionally. You will be a better human being if you embrace the beauty and emotion that the field of art can contribute to your wellbeing and growth.

Take advantage of the art program you are exposed to and allow your own creative juices to flow. You will become more of a mature adult if you open yourself to this magical area of learning.

I have enclosed the two paintings your grandmother and I did at a recent art class. We hope you enjoy them. Don't judge them but appreciate the fact that two "elderly" people made an attempt to feed the satisfaction of creating something that they felt as they viewed a still life project that was organized for them to reflect upon.

Art may not be as exciting to you as in the same way or manner in which the world of sports might appeal to you. However, may I remind you that in order to be a complete individual, you need to be open to all avenues of learning. Give art a chance and I am certain that you will be a "richer" and better person.

Love,
Papa & Nana
February 24, 2014

CHARITY

Dear Jaden,

I hope you enjoyed your birthday and that you shared it in many happy events with your friends and parents. It is difficult to imagine that you are now 10 years of age. Time really flies by quickly and we are all pleased with how well you are doing in all the activities that are part of your life. You have a lot to look forward to as you grow and mature.

Today, we will look at the word "charitable" or "charity" and discuss how that concept can become part of your lifestyle even if you don't have the funds (money) to give to worthwhile causes. First of all, charity doesn't have to mean only the giving of money to those less fortunate than yourself. Actually the giving of yourself to help others is far more meaningful in this regard.

Learning to be charitable in the giving of your time and energy to help others offers you the distinctive opportunity to become a better person. Some people are fortunate to have been born with certain gifts (good health, supportive parents in a wholesome home environment, intelligence and specific physical and intellectual skills to build upon, etc. etc.). Others are not that blessed and will need the support and kindness of others to take advantage of the many things that provide for a happy and productive life.

It is important for you to learn how to "give" of yourself to others who are less fortunate. There are so many ways you can incorporate that into your life. There are certain jobs and professions that are specifically geared to provide for others. Teaching, social work and the medical profession are some of the examples of how people devote their lives to support and nurture others. However, the ultimate avenue open to all of us is the manner in which we conduct our lives. A key component of your daily doings should be clearly observed in how you relate to others (family, friends and all who are part of your life as you mature.). Being sensitive and understanding of the needs of others will make you a more complete, wholesome human being. You need to learn to give of your time, energy and love to the many who are part of your daily life! The more people you relate to in positive ways, the richer your life will become and the greater your legacy will be when you are gone.

If someday you are fortunate to have been able to accumulate a lot of wealth, you should be willing and able to support worthwhile organizations and charities with the financial means to help them provide for others in need. However, money is a small part of what would make you a charitable, giving person. Being helpful and understanding of the needs of the many people who will come in and out of your life and being supportive of whatever issues they may present will endear you to them as feeling and kind as they relate to you as a person.

104

Thus, I end with this guideline for you to follow, "the kind of life you live will determine how charitable your existence on earth has been."

Love,
Papa & Nana
March 1, 2014

THE COLOR GREEN

Dear Jaden,

Now that spring (my favorite time of the year) is here, I would like to share my feelings about the color green.

The color green is the color of balance, harmony and growth. Psychologically, the color green reflects a great balance of the heart and the emotions which helps to create a sense of equilibrium (evenness) between the head and the heart.

The color of Spring, of renewal and rebirth is green. It renews and restores depleted energy. It is a peaceful approach away from the stresses of modern living, restoring us back to a sense of wellbeing. That is why there is so much of the relaxing color on the earth and why we need to keep it that way.

Green is an emotionally positive color, giving us the ability to love and nurture ourselves and others unconditionally. It is a natural peacemaker and something that adds richly to our lives.

I am hopeful that you will visit us this summer in Sag Harbor and meet all my "green, colorful" friends who are presently breaking through the ground now and will be available to greet you and love you with no conditions during your visit to the Seidman Garden.

Now, a small response to your recent experience at school regarding changing your assigned mathematics group. You should look upon this as a positive move which will allow you to meet a challenge that will help to make you a more complete and capable student. From what I gather, you have the ability to be in the more advanced grouping in math. What you need is the motivation and appropriate study skills to meet this issue. Taking your time to complete directions of the teacher and following them completely and asking questions if you are having difficulty with the assignment, will be of great value to you in being successful in this complex area of learning.

You have the intelligence and understanding to meet this challenge and now you have to apply a mature approach to reach your goal. The ball is in your "ball park". Work at it and do your best. Just apply yourself and good things will happen.

Love,
Your "green" Papa & Nana
April 30, 2014

CURIOSITY

Dear Jaden,

Today I would like to arouse your interest in the important human trait called "curiosity". Being curious is an innate (inborn) common feeling that we all enjoy. In my mind, it is those who are curious and who act with inquisitive minds who learn more about themselves as well as others, and develop more completely as caring people in our society.

Asking questions and exploring all avenues of learning helps to satisfy the curious mind. I sincerely feel that you possess that potential learning skill and desire to grow as a person. I would like to take this time to suggest certain paths that you can follow to help satisfy this need to learn more about the world around you.

First of all, you must be willing to ask questions of everyone you meet and know. This will include your parents, your teachers, your friends and your family including those people who come and go in your life. It is quite appropriate to admit that you don't know everything (obviously) but that you are interested in learning about all sorts of things to help enrich your life and make you a more knowledgeable person. You will discover that people, in general, will respond willingly to guide you in your genuine thirst for learning.

I have discovered that most people are interested in sharing their "story" with you. Of course, there will be times (on rare occasion) when you confront a "grouch" (an irritable person) with issues on the process of communication and social behavior who might not be responsive to you. This will be the rare occurrence and it should not discourage you.

I have discovered that most people are interested in sharing their "story"...

May I also encourage you to use a tape recorder to capture the words of those you are seeking information from. For example, your Nana (grandmother) has a very interesting and meaningful story to share with you about her life as a child. You could learn much about her circumstances relating to World War II and how it affected her life. This audio technique could be used with lots of people you interview to help you gather information and maintain records of these conversations. It is a great technique called "oral history".

In addition to questioning others, you must always search within yourself answers to the many issues that you will be facing as you grow up. Using books, reference material, the internet, libraries and a host of other sources to open your mind to the world of knowledge is necessary.

Become a "learner" who wants to grow intellectually. My letter to you merely opens up a few avenues for you to follow. I wish you a long, successful journey in your quest for knowledge and more importantly for your understanding and appreciation for all people. Happy learning!

Love,
Papa and Nana
December 3, 2013

Dear Papa,

I am curious about many things. I am curious about adulthood and the freedom that comes with it. What makes adulthood so special? Is there anything that really stands out about being an adult other than height? Is adulthood exhilarating? Does it take you through a ride, and blow your mind? I would also like to know what it was like to grow up in a crowded city (New York) after your parents had sadly passed away. How did you make it in New York? I know you wanted to be a baseball player. Was it hard to deal with hopes and dreams at that time?

I am also curious about what it is like to climb a mountain. The interesting part of climbing the mountain is what lies ahead. How does getting to the summit feel? What are the feelings that run through the head of the climber? What makes the experience so memorable? What makes the feeling of accomplishment so great? The reason I ask these questions is because I am young, and I have not had enough time on earth to experience these things.

Different ages have different levels of curiosity. Kids dream big while adults have dreamed big already. I think that there is some part of them that wants to keep learning and another part that does not want to learn and thinks that they have learned enough.

There will always be a part of me that wants to stay curious. Seizing the moment and staying optimistic is important. Nobody will learn everything. After all there is soooooooooooooo much to learn. But it is better to learn a lot than to learn a little. Even though you may not know everything, you will still have much knowledge.

You are only given about a 100 billion brain cells. They can't reproduce, but you can stretch them. If you keep learning new things, read, and stay curious that will stretch your brain cells which will make you have more brain power. This may be able to give older folks more brain power and keep more people curious which may inspire people to learn new things about the world and beyond.

I talked a little bit about how a younger person like me views curiosity. Do you agree with what I said about curiosity? Do you still have the need to keep learning and stay curious?

Sincerely,
Jaden

Dear Jaden,

I truly enjoyed your recent letter regarding your response to my written communication pertaining to the important human trait called "curiosity". Your letter revealed a lot of good thought and feeling about your understanding of "curiosity " and it stimulated many questions and intelligent insights on your part that I will attempt to respond to in the hope and expectation that my sharing with you will prove to be productive for the both of us. Your growth as a "thinking and questioning young man" reflects a maturity level well beyond your eleven years on earth. I am very proud of you and I remain confident that our exchange of letters will be beneficial for both of us.

Your question about "what makes adulthood so special?" deserves a thoughtful response. The only way adulthood can become special is when the individual (you) recognizes that the movement from childhood to adulthood will include many "ups and downs". Thus it becomes a process of taking advantage of the many positives one has in his life span and seeks to appreciate how to gain knowledge from the negatives in life by learning and acquiring the ability to turn these actions into learning experiences. Achieving adulthood doesn't mean attaining a certain height in stature, as you suggested, but it does mean developing a maturity level that enables you to make decisions and perform deeds that will make your life and the others who surround you more meaningful and worthwhile. Adulthood (maturity) is more than physical growth. Yes, it can be exhilarating as you mentioned in you letter, but more importantly it will present a number of challenges that must be met with positive efforts on your part. Growing to adulthood is a difficult process, but it can "blow your mind" (your words) if you successfully meet the challenges you will face.

You asked how it was to live in a crowded city like New York and what effect the early deaths of my parents had upon me during my "growing" years. I've always loved NYC because it is a huge place where someone can find opportunities aplenty, where one can lose oneself when facing the sadness of lost loved ones. Sometimes adversity (difficulty) can make a person stronger, particularly if the attachments to family and friends remain strong. My parents passed away too early in life, but I have always felt their presence and support. Having hopes and dreams always remain alive if one remains motivated and eager to grow and develop as a person. That's what adulthood is all about.

Your curiosity about what it would be like to climb a mountain that has meaning for you and it is feelings like those you expressed that will serve you well as you grow and develop. There is a need for all of us to climb mountains, whether they be real or are found in other obstacles that challenge us as human beings. You are young at this point in your life, but you will in time

110

develop the ability to enjoy the feeling of accomplishment as you mature and set goals for yourself.

You are correct in feeling that "kids" dream big, but it need not stop there. Your dreams should become even larger as you age and all of that will become possible because you possess the capacity to develop an insatiable (huge) appetite to continue to learn and grow during your entire life, even when you reach your late eighties, like your grandfather. Your desire to appreciate the need to continue learning, to use your given brain power regardless of your age level has great merit. In addition, your thoughts about curiosity and the ability to grow at all ages makes me feel very positive about my own continued development. I look forward to growing and maturing alongside of you.

Love,
Papa & Nana
November 11, 2015

CURRENT EVENTS

Dear Jaden,

Your mother and father recently shared with me that you have expressed some interest and concern about the present world situation as it relates to the events in the Middle East and Africa and the frightening growth of "terrorism" throughout the world. I don't know if I can fully allay (remove or lessen) all your fears but I will try to address some of the issues you posed to help put things in proper prospective (as they exist) according to my view of the distressing problems you presented.

First of all, I would like to address the role that the media (television, radio, internet and all forms of written and verbal coverage) has played in this area, while the overall issue of terrorism and war in the Middle East and parts of Africa, etc. is a concern to all of us, the fervor (enthusiasm) that the media has injected into this disturbing picture of the conditions in our world had led to a very disturbing and often distorted view of the environment in which we live. I don't desire to overemphasize this point but I do wish to call your attention to it. To give you an example of what I mean, I refer you to the "Ebola" epidemic which was forecast to be coming to the USA by the frenzy (excitement) provided by many of the media sources available to us. It certainly was a major issue for all of us but it turned out to be less of a threat than originally envisioned (viewed). What I am trying to relate to you is that it is absolutely necessary that you and the rest of us become more knowledgeable about the world around us and not only rely on the media coverage of any event that is of importance to our wellbeing. We need to rely upon many sources of information and not be led by media which can be biased and misleading.

My thoughts as a young boy were very much the same as yours are now.

Since I was born (only 86 years ago) I have lived through a great many disastrous and earth shattering experiences that threaten the welfare of the world and its vast population, some examples include World War I & II, the "cold war" with Russia, the Korean conflict, the war in Vietnam and so many smaller wars over the years which leads us to the present wars in the Middle East (Iraq, etc.) and the problem of world-wide terrorism we face today. The history of our great world is full of tragic events (from ancient history to present day) which have lessened (diminished) the lives of millions and millions of people who have preceded (came before) us. It is a sad reality, but we need to look forward to a better and safer future for you and other young people. How can we accomplish that?

112

I have great hope for your generation to help reverse the flow of history as it now exists. You and your friends have a real chance to eradicate (remove) the climate that has been responsible for our present state. You, and the many young people like you, are growing up in an environment that promotes equality and respect for the rights of others regardless of their differences, sexual orientation and all the many individual traits that allow us to be a rich, complex society. We have made some strides (steps) in that direction but unfortunately we still have a segment of our population that has not allowed us, and the world around us, to grow to meet the responsibility of making life a fulfilling and productive experience for all.

My world of today is still trying to remove the ignorance that surrounds such issues as women's rights, sexual orientation differences, effects of climate changes, evolution, education and economical issues that have plagued our country and encouraged a lack of empathy for others. Your generation will gain from our errors and work toward equal opportunity for all. We will never again enter into a war with a spurious (false) premise, as we did in the Iraq conflict, and create an atmosphere that allowed the ISIS state (terrorists) to be created. I have great hopes that your generation would gain knowledge from this experience and never repeat it in the future.

In time, we will find the means to abate (resolve) this awful conflict we now face. We always have met this kind of challenge in the past. My expectation and hope is that when you reach adulthood your world will be safer and better because of the input and efforts of people like you and the other members of your generation. Each generation makes progress and my expectation is that your group will have a greater potential to make the world a better and more wholesome place to enjoy all the fruits of life.

I urge you not to fret (worry) about the world's situation as it now appears. We will work through it with some loss and upset but we will survive. It is more important that you, and the millions of others who will join you in 15-20 years, learn from what has taken place in the past and create something that is nurturing and receptive to all people.   113

My thoughts as a young boy were very much the same as yours are now. However, I feel confident that you and your generation will do a better job in making the world a better place for your children in the future. Good Luck!!

Love,
Papa & Nana
March 1, 2015

FAMILY

Dear Jaden,

Today I would like to share my thoughts and feelings about the role family plays in our lives. The importance of family and the significance this body of people have in molding you as a person is a major factor in determining who you will be as a functioning person in our society.

Obviously, the most important people in your life will be your parents. They will provide the important ingredients that will promote the foundation to enable you to develop into a caring, loving and successful man. They nurture you, feed you and meet all your physical, social and emotional needs as you develop and grow up. How well they perform those responsibilities will determine what kind of person you will be. I trust that you know that you are in "good hands" and that they will do their best to ensure that your movement and growth from infancy to adulthood will be accompanied with much love, patience, and support to make this transition and process as positive as possible. This upbringing and commitment on their part will become the foundation that will support your entire life. Once again, I have to relate to you that you are "one lucky" young man.

This foundation is enhanced by the many other members of your family that encompass your life. Cousins, uncles, aunts, nephews, nieces, brothers, sisters and, of course, grandparents, are part of the complex of both families (your mother's and father's) that are additional support structures in your development. They will remain as permanent fixtures in your existence and will also interact with you on a positive level as you grow up. Some will be more endearing than others (like your grandfather "Papa") and on the whole, they will provide good feelings and care for you during the coming years. You are a mixture of the "genes" from both families and if you are lucky (and you are) then the combination of those inherited traits will serve you well during your voyage through life.

I would like to suggest that you look closely at your total family and love them for their strengths, their weaknesses, and similarities and most importantly accept them as major players in your life. You are very fortunate to be surrounded by a diversified, intelligent and caring group of people. Your love and interaction with them will only make you more complete and capable as a person.

Your family loves you and you are blessed to have them in your life.

Love,
Papa & Nana
May 1, 2015

Dear Jaden,

My topic (subject) for today is "why you should love flowers and all the wonderful things that grow in the earth." As you know, I love gardening and watching my flowers, trees, bushes, and even vegetables grow and flourish during the warm months of spring and summer. This has become one of the great joys of my life. There is no greater sense of achievement and accomplishment than planting a seed and watching it develop into a beautiful plant over time. It is similar to the experience of observing a boy like you develop from a "seed" into a mature, handsome man as the seasons of each year change and provide you with the time and support to move into the stages of adulthood.

Let's look closely at how plants and human beings have so much in common. All forms of plants need water, food or nutrition, care or support and the appropriate time to grow and develop to their full potential. Planting a seed requires much of the same kind of care that is necessary in the raising of a human baby. It needs to be fed and nurtured, in addition to being given the time to adjust to its environment. That was the exact situation you faced when you were born. Not all plants and humans grow at the same rate. Some will be tall and others will be short. They will be different colors, shapes, sizes and in many ways evoke different emotions, from those (animate and inanimate) around them. Some plants attract insects, others attract birds and animals but all of them (very much like humans) strive for independence, despite their need for support from all different sources to survive. As you can see, they are not that very different from humans in that regard.

Many plants (perennials) come back year after year and show new growth or additional plants which is similar to our human development process when a baby is born in the family. It was the same when you were born and the Miller-Seidman family added a new bud to the "clan."

116

Plants, like people, are beautiful to look at and they add much to our environment There is no greater joy than watching a plant grow and develop. The best comparison I can make is the one I loved making to others when I served as head of a school. To me, each child was like a plant in need of a proper and inviting atmosphere in which to grow and prosper. An environment that would include love, understanding and a time to grow at their own level of development for each child.

I am hopeful that someday you will grow your own gardens. One garden devoted to your family of humans (parents, relatives, friends and others) which will help you be a better person because of the knowledge you have gained from recognizing how really difficult it is to appreciate something that asks little of you but gives you such great rewards in return. It is difficult to learn humanity and be humble. Happy gardening!!

Love,
Papa & Nana
January 25, 2014

HUMOR

Dear Jaden,

Today I am going to share some thoughts I have about something that we both have in common. It is called "a sense of humor" and it is important that we learn how to use this gift and not abuse it.

Everyone loves a person who has a good sense of humor, who knows how to use it wisely without offending others. Being humorous (funny and clever) means that you can use words well. It is a skill that will make people like you and feel good about listening to you when you speak. However, it also carries a responsibility that requires a sensitivity on your part to the feelings of others. Let me give you an example of that. A boy or girl who jokes around and acts foolishly in the classroom draws a lot of attention from his teacher and classmates. This activity can take away precious learning time and can be looked upon as a negative experience by everyone in the classroom.

Humor should be used as a positive force to make people feel good about themselves and, of course, you. All people like to laugh and they all enjoy funny stories and jokes. The key to good humor revolves around timing and how carefully worded or orchestrated humor is presented.

You should not make fun of others if you are not willing to have them "poke" fun at you. The best jokes or stories are the ones you tell about yourself which allow your friends to see you as vulnerable and provides them with the opportunity to identify with you and your humorous dilemmas (problems).

Allow me to encourage you to use your clever sense of humor wisely and with care. Laugh with your friends and family and offer them the opportunity to laugh at you. They will like you more if they recognize that you can also laugh at yourself. Don't be conceited or full of yourself in your daily activities with others, but do show that unique side of yourself that is accepting of your own limitations and actions. This should be recognized in your behavior and understanding of the world in which you are pleased to be an active participant.

Good humor will endear you to others and will make you a dear and special friend to the many people in your life. Unfortunately, there will be some sadness in your life but your ability to take something positive and even humorous from the most difficult happenings, will make you a more complete and understanding person. Use your precious sense of humor wisely and continue to love life.

Love,
Papa & Nana
118   March 14, 2014

Dear Jaden,

I hope you enjoyed your vacation and that you had a great time in Hawaii. It is really good to have vacation time and the opportunity of rest and relaxation after a period of hard work and effort at school or work. All of this has been "baked in" or integrated into the fabric of every school system in the United States and, while I believe that the concept of vacation time is a good one, I also think that someone has to reevaluate some of the practices that are followed today in setting up calendars for the school year in need of some review and change.

Did you know that when the United States was originally created the main industry of this newly formed country was agriculture (farming). This meant that the land (farms) was cared for and worked on by the families who lived on this land. The children of these families were needed to seed and plant the fields in the spring and to care for the land and harvest the crops (food) in the summer and fall seasons. As a result, the schools in those days accommodated these families and provided long vacation periods during these seasons for the children to enable them to assist their parents with the task of farming the land and support their families financially.

The development of the "Industrial Revolution" in the 19th century changed the landscape of our country in many ways by moving our agricultural world into an industrial society, with the majority of working opportunities (jobs, employment) centered in factories, offices, etc. located in small and large cities throughout a different United States of America. Over the last 100 plus years we have transformed our country from an environment that relied on farming as a main source of income to one that is predominately industrial. Yet we still follow the same calendar on a yearly basis that was originated when we were a young emerging country of mostly farmers.

I personally feel that we need to rethink the country-wide school calendars and adapt to our present needs as a technological and industrial society. We need to look at the large number of vacation days that schools provide each year and extend the school year and, as a result, add days and hours of school instructional time to help all students reach the challenges of the explosion of knowledge and new technological skills that are now part of our new educational world. It is a daunting (difficult) goal to achieve but we must revisit the organization of the educational system that presently exists.

Now I am not suggesting that we do away with vacation time in schools. On the contrary, I am recommending that a revision be made to cut back on the excessive time devoted to time out of school and allow students to enjoy more time during extended school time to meet our present educational challenges. This can be done while still allowing students appropriate vacation "down time" for the rest and play. I hope you agree.

Love,
Papa & Nana
April 10, 2014

Dear Jaden,

     I hope this letter finds you in good health and that you are enjoying receiving my weekly letters. Today, I am going to share with you my understanding and appreciation of how "music plays an important role in your life and how it should be incorporated into your daily activities."

     The love for music can make your life richer and more meaningful. It offers emotional experiences that run the gamut (range) from happiness and joy to calmness and even sadness. Some music can make you feel happy and bursting with energy while other musical experiences can make you feel reflective and often self-searching in exploring the different emotions you are feeling. This is accomplished as you listen to the magical notes that reach you ears and hopefully your soul.

     You are indeed fortunate. You possess a God-given talent in this important aspect (part) of your life. It is clear that you enjoy singing and my expectation is that someday you will master the art of playing a musical instrument which will also help to enrich your life. Your love for music is easily discerned (observed) in the different musical events you perform at school and sometimes even at home (where you think no one is listening). Your parents and others are provided with a brief view of your talent and joy for this creative area of learning.

     There are times when listening to music can bring tears to your eyes, especially when you hear something that connects your inner feelings to something, someone or some event that meant a great deal to you.

     There are other times when the music you are listening to makes you smile and feel happy thoughts and emotions because you relate it to a joyful experience in your life.

     Your parents (particularly your mother) have always included music in their lives. You should continue to follow their lead and allow it to be an integral (key) part of your life. It will make you a better person and a more complete human being.

You have many more songs to sing and lots of musical experiences to look forward to as you grow into adulthood. Follow the music in your heart, share it with others and encourage it to play a supportive and loving role in your life.

Keep singing and continue loving music for it will make you a richer and happier person.

Love,
Papa & Nana
February 7, 2014

READING

Dear Jaden,

Today's letter will be devoted to "learning how to spend leisure time wisely and why reading has to be an important part of that concept." In other words, reading should be a key activity in your leisure (recreational) life.

As a young man growing up you will be a very busy person trying to fit into your daily routine all the many things you need to do to meet the responsibilities you have to complete each day. I am referring to the things you need to do at home, at school and in meeting all of the assigned chores you have to perform each day for yourself and others. Fortunately for you, there will be some time when you will be given the opportunity to engage in activities that you love and take great pleasure in doing. There will be time for you to enjoy the sports that you play and follow, time to play computer games and involve yourself in the world of technology and, of course, time to just relax and gather yourself together and do some insightful thinking.

Allow me to encourage you to pursue another leisure time activity that will play a major role in making you a successful, knowledgeable and thoughtful person as you move from childhood into the formidable task of becoming a productive, thinking adult. You must find time to read each day. It can be for pleasure, it can be for gaining information and understanding the world around you, and most importantly it can merely be done to make you a more complete and informed person who can speak with knowledge, understanding and passion about the world in which you live and contribute to each day that you are blessed to be on earth. Make reading an integral (central portion) of your life. Almost all of the successful people in our world are those who are well-read and who are open to learning more about themselves and the emotions and feelings that guide their daily lives and support their relationships with others. I am pleased that you are showing signs of becoming an avid reader now that you are reaching your tenth birthday. There is much for you to learn and even more for you to share with others.

I am not suggesting that you take time away from the many things that you love to do but I am recommending that you manage your time so that reading each day becomes a permanent part of your lifestyle. Life reflects all of the choices that each of us makes as we develop and mature. How you use the time given to you on earth will determine who you will become as a person. I trust that you will make the decisions that will serve you best.

Love,
Papa & Nana
February 15, 2014

Dear Jaden,

Now that your grandparents have finally settled down for the coming winter season in "sunny" Florida, I thought it might be a good idea to once again revisit with you the true significance of the coming Thanksgiving holiday, and what really needs to be emphasized by all who share in the celebration of this joyful holiday.

Let's put aside the "trappings" (for example, the sharing of the turkey feast, the autumn leaves, the big sales in the many department store the big parade and the historical review of the Pilgrims and Native Americans getting together to peacefully enjoy the sharing of a meal and learning to appreciate each others' values and customs) and spend some time thinking about giving thanks for the many things in your young life that makes you such a fortunate young boy with a potentially bright and enriching future.

Those who are blessed (you) should recognize that learning to give and share will make them better people.

You should now take the time at this point in your young life to evaluate what the concept of "Thanksgiving" means to you. In other words, what are you thankful for and how can you best express your gratefulness for all the positive components (parts) of your first ten years of your life.

Obviously I want you to enjoy your Thanksgiving holiday but I would also like you to move beyond that feeling and think carefully about how you can give real "thanks" for all the wonderful experiences that have been a keen part of your life thus far. It is important that you express your sincere appreciation to those who have provided so much for your welfare. I would like you to think about how you can reciprocate to them in a fashion that is giving and caring. This positive action on your part would be important in revealing who you are as a person.

124

The expression of deep love and empathy you have for your family, friends and all others in your life will be the most suitable approach for you to express your appreciation in celebrating this holiday. In addition, you need to learn to share this love and good feeling with others who are less fortunate and in need. Those who are blessed (you) should recognize that learning to give and share will make them better people. You have that potential and I hope you enjoy the coming Thanksgiving holiday in a manner that brings joy and good feeling to all who are fortunate to share in your life.

Love,
Papa & Nana
November 7, 2014

INTROSPECTION

Dear Jaden,

Today I would like to introduce you to a new word that I strongly urge you add to your vocabulary. The word is "introspective" and it means to look "inside" of yourself and attempt to learn more completely who you are as a person. It is a difficult vocabulary word for you at this stage in your life, but it is an important concept for you to embrace and utilize (use) as a means to know yourself so that you can function effectively as a contributing member in the world that you will live, work, love in and hopefully make better. To be introspective means to possess the ability to look at oneself and recognize the strengths, weaknesses, needs, passions and desires that are part of you which offer you the opportunity to hold a complete appreciation for the environment that nurtures your very being. As a result of this effort, it will open all kinds of opportunities for you to understand yourself better and allow you to appreciate and provide for the needs of others who will be part of your life. Allow me to emphasize this point: know yourself well and that attribute will help make you a positive force among the many people you will "touch" during your years on earth. Being comfortable with who you are as a person opens many opportunities for you to grow and develop a legacy of love and compassion for others.

This does not mean that you have to be perfect at all times. Even your mother can't reach that high a pinnacle. You will make mistakes but you should learn from them. If you judge yourself too harshly then you will carry that over to the relationships you have with the people in your life. You have to recognize and accept the fact that you can't know and do everything and, like everyone else, you have your limitations. Keeping that in mind will enable you to cherish the many things that you and others can do so well.

I strongly urge you not to be judgmental in your communications with others. You should set an example of acceptance and understanding in your relationships with them and use the same standards that you set for yourself in your dealings with all segments of our population. If you have the good fortune to emerge as a leader in your chosen work or profession, it will become incumbent (necessary) for you to set an example in your work ethic, personal relationships, and your appreciation of the differences (strengths and weaknesses) of each person to help create an environment that promotes growth and good feeling among the members of your immediate community.

Keep evaluating what you have accomplished and recognize that you will always need the support of many to be successful in whatever endeavor you choose to enter. It you are pleased and satisfied with what you have accomplished, remember to acknowledge those who worked alongside you and slowly "raised the bar" to move up the ladder. Use their support with your future endeavors to succeed. Recognize that you didn't reach your goals without the goodwill of others. No one achieves without some assistance and support.

I would also like to remind you that being a "successful" person in life includes more than your achievements at work. You need to live a well-rounded life. Hopefully you will enjoy your schooling experiences, find love and happiness with someone who will share in the joy of raising a family, and enjoy an enriched lifestyle that includes all the magical opportunities such as music, theater, fine arts and culture, sports, technology and, most importantly, the love and respect of family, friends and fellow workers.

Enjoy what is to come and keep exploring all the possibilities available that will make you a better person. This can only be accomplished within yourself as you develop an "introspective" style of living. You posses all the ingredients to be successful.

Best wishes & Love,
Papa & Nana
August 15, 2014

ACKNOWLEDGEMENTS

We would love to thank teachers everywhere that encourage students to write and explore their inner voices without judgment. Andrew Wiener has been that truly extraordinary teacher and we sincerely thank him for being an influential and creative force in Jaden's life. Additionally, we offer our heartfelt thanks to Lisa Occhipinti for her endless support in helping to organize and design our book.

Above all, we want to thank Wayne, (best dad and husband ever) who would scan every letter after reading so that we could have a record of this special correspondence. His love and humorous approach to each conversation was and is an enormous part of the heart of this project.

And of course, our amazing family, Lillian, Lee, Chester, Connie, Leo, Carol, Howard, Hayley, Arianna, Mason, Michael, Leslie, Shelly, Adam, Jenny, Isabella, Valentina, Jake, Paul, Gil, Harriet and of course, special mention to Nana (Diana) who helped read each letter and offered her comments before they were mailed to Jaden.

Finally, I want to thank Papa, my dad and mentor. I treasure our conversations and feel blessed that I was the "mom" in the middle of the correspondence with Jaden. I look forward to many more letters and discussions about the color green, flowers, bullies and politics!

–RM

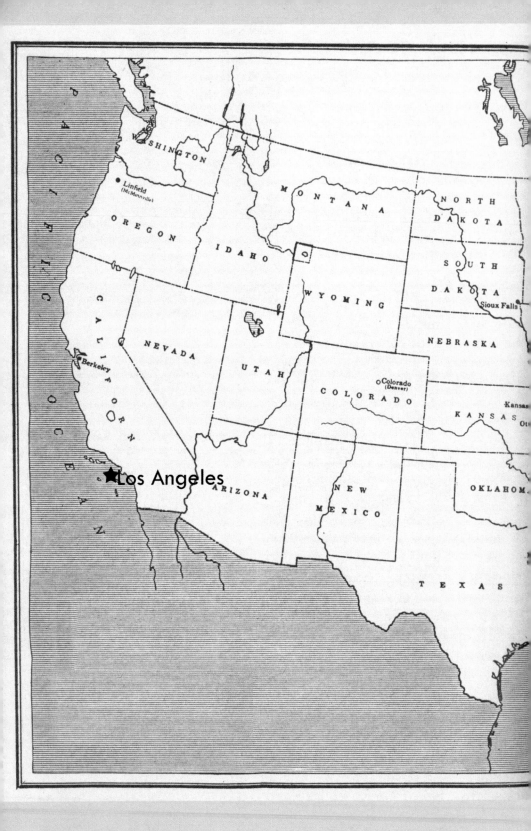

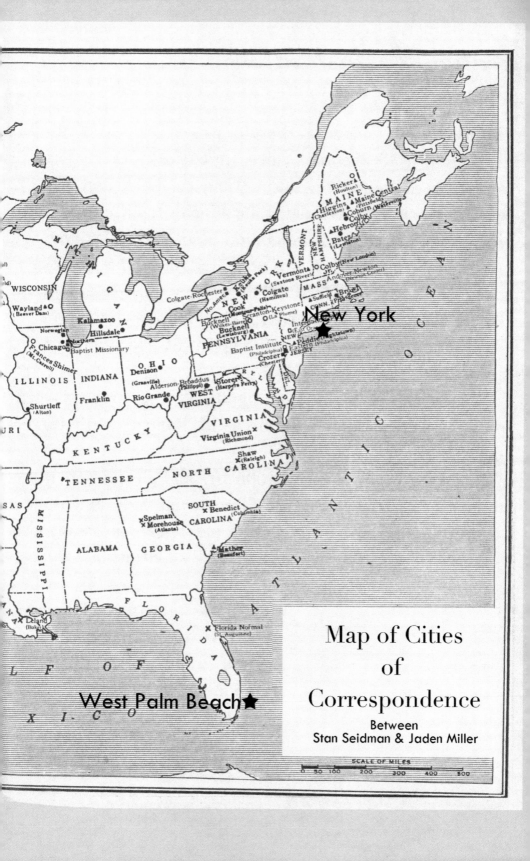

New York

West Palm Beach

Map of Cities
of
Correspondence
Between
Stan Seidman & Jaden Miller

SCALE OF MILES
0   50 100   200   300   400   500

larger + larger each day. your vocabulary keeps getting ... First of
charming "performer" and personality. I am very ... tempt to sh...
proud of you and love you dearly. ... over 60 years
I + is rewarding and wonderful that we ... a subsequen...
have established such a strong bond between us. I ... you my feelings
look forward to seeing you often and watching you ... as a young pe...
grow into a very special young man. ... as a mature ...
your "NaNa" and I will be there ... 87 years on e...
to share the coming new year with you and we are ... to that numb...
looking to enjoy some more hot chocolate with you.
Tell your parents not to work too hard. They are ... I chos...
doing a great job with you!! ... this letter b...
Love, ... much m...
Grandpa + NaNa ... onal

...speaking ...
...th you ...day.
...your speaking ...for
...is very impressive and
...a boy your age and
...I love how well
...you enjoy "flowers".
...Enjoy all the
...plants + flowers but
...don't abuse them. you
...e very ... gentle with

Jaden Miller
724

3.7 USA

5/18/15
Re: The Loss of a

Dear Jaden,
I just learned from your mother
...me very upset when you witnessed
...peared when she shared with you
...ayley's sister was terminally ill
...prospect of death at such
...your emotional response w...
...this unhappy occurrence
...e to share my thoughts
...an eventuality that a
...having an under...
...an important on

STANLEY SEIDMAN

Dear Jaden,
I am enclosing some
letters I received from children
like you. Some day you will write
...own letters.
...I hope you enjoy my
...Love Poppy...

...express my
...because I want y
...e (which we all must fac
...e on this earth to de...
...ept. It is vital for yo...
...stand why it is so impo...
...e of love for yourself and oth...
...sincere attempt to make the wo...
...llow you. this approach
...worthwhile

Proof

Made in the USA
Charleston, SC
10 March 2016